BREAKTHROUGH

BREAKTHROUGH

Insights of the Great Religious Discoverers

Clifford G. Hospital

ORBIS BOOKS

Maryknoll, New York 10545

The Catholic Foreign Mission Society of America (Maryknoll) recruits and trains people for overseas missionary service. Through Orbis Books Maryknoll aims to foster the international dialogue that is essential to mission. The books published, however, reflect the opinions of their authors and are not meant to represent the official position of the society.

Except where otherwise noted, quotations from the Bible are from the *New English Bible*, New York, Oxford University Press, 1972. Quotations from the Quran are from N.J. Dawood, *The Koran*, Harmondsworth, Middlesex, Penguin, 1959. Bibliographical details of translations of other foundational religious texts are given where they occur.

Copyright © 1985 by Clifford G. Hospital
Published by Orbis Books, Maryknoll, NY 10545
Manufactured in the United States of America
All rights reserved

Manuscript Editor: William E. Jerman

Library of Congress Cataloging in Publication Data

Hospital, Clifford.
  Breakthrough: insights of the great religious discoverers.

  Bibliography: p.
  1. Religions. 2. Sacred books. 3. Religious
biography. I. Title.
BL80.2.H67 1985   291   85-5135
ISBN 0-88344-206-X (pbk.)

For
Janette, Geoffrey, and Cressida

CONTENTS

PREFACE

This book attempts a new approach to the major religious traditions of humankind. It presents what are arguably the most significant figures of religious history as religious discoverers whose insights have been the heritage of us all. The vision of each discoverer has been portrayed in the interplay between the basic teachings on the one hand and the life story on the other. (In each case, of course, it is the basic teaching and the life story as they have been developed by those who responded to that vision.)

I have attempted to capture the flavor of the teachings in a manner that textbooks giving an account of the history of the world religions rarely attempt. It is common to look at such figures strictly in terms of their historical and cultural context—with a major interest in the dynamics of historical development. A difficulty with such an approach is that at the end of the endeavor the student is often left observing a set of quite profound materials as a remote curiosity.

Although not wanting to underplay the importance of historical investigation, I have attempted to go further. I have tried to develop a hermeneutic that allows the basic texts to speak with some directness to contemporary human beings. Thus I have attempted to hear what is being said within the specific cultural contexts, as far as they are made available to us from historical scholarship; and then to present the vision in a mode less culturally confined, so that readers may understand on their own terms what is being said. And because the historical details to the extent that we know them are available, in lesser or greater complexity, in a large number of works, I have not concentrated on them except insofar as a consideration of them is valuable in elucidating for us the religious vision of the figures concerned.

It will be observed that the religious traditions related to each of these central figures have very complex histories, evidence a great variety of religious styles, and are replete with disputes about numerous issues. This I do not deny. Yet I am persuaded that in each of the traditions there are certain symbols and teachings that are basic if not normative for the tradition; and I believe that what I present here via these central figures in almost every case comes close to being an accepted, authentic core of the vision of life of the respective tradition.

My intention, then, has been to present an interesting and readable text in which these religious discoverers are treated directly but also at some depth. I have also intended that it be a book that raises questions, not the least being the extent to which the discoveries of these creative figures are available to the global village in which we live and in what way they can together contribute to human community at its widest.

First presented some years ago to the Kingston Lay School of Theology, the central ideas of this book have been revised as I have presented them to successive groups of students in an introductory course on the religious history of humankind at Queen's University. My thanks go out to students too numerous to name for comments and questions that have helped me to formulate my ideas more clearly. I am also indebted to colleagues at Queen's and elsewhere who have read the text in whole or part and have provided encouragement and helpful comments: William James, Robert Bater, John Cook, Elias Andrews, Dennis Hudson, and Herbert Basser. My wife, Janette, has helped me improve the literary quality of the writing, and Dorothy Schweder has been patient and efficient in typing and retyping successive versions of the text. To all of these I wish to express my heartfelt thanks.

The ideas that I have put together in my own way are, of course, not all my own. I have heard and read a great deal about the figures whose life stories and teachings are presented here, and I have assimilated ideas into my own thinking to the extent that it is now impossible to trace the origins of much that I have said. Some of those to whom I am indebted are included in the notes, and the works mentioned there may be regarded also as a suggested short list for further reading. But there are others not specifically referred to there who have been important to me in the formation of my ideas. My interest in the comparative, historical study of religion was stimulated initially by E.L. Allen and Robert W. Fulcher at the University of Queensland in Australia; I spent a term in the School of Theology at Claremont where I took courses with Virginia Corwin and Floyd Ross. Some of the thinking in which they guided me is reflected in what I have written here.

Most significantly, however, as a doctoral candidate at Harvard University I studied with Wilfred Cantwell Smith. As a student and teaching assistant I attended successive years of classes in his introductory course on the history of religion. Many of the ideas presented in the following pages—probably even more than I am myself now aware—were stimulated by his remarkably thoughtful presentations. And although the overall view of what I am about has been worked out in a dialogue with a variety of thinkers, of them all it is he whose vision of the whole has been most pervasive and persuasive for me. To him in his sympathy, understanding, and wisdom, I am profoundly indebted.

INTRODUCTION

In 1980 a young man began walking across the continent of North America. A Canadian, he decided to cross it at its widest—from Nova Scotia to Vancouver. That somebody should attempt this feat is nothing remarkable. In these days when persons think up new records to break so that they can have their names in Guinness, we have seen people cycle and walk and roller-skate and balloon across this continent and perform similar feats in other parts of the world.

What was remarkable, however, about this young fellow, Terry Fox, was that only one of the legs he was using to walk across North America was his own. Terry had lost his other leg to cancer.

He began his marathon of hope intent on raising $1 million for the fight against cancer. At the beginning few noticed him, but then as he hobbled through Quebec and Ontario Canadians began to take note of his odyssey, his heroic journey, and they began to contribute to his vision.

But then his walk stopped: the stump of his amputated leg had become a raw sore. Then it was discovered the cancer had spread to his lungs. In his inability to proceed, however, the full heroism of his journey became evident and the public responded. In a "Telethon for Terry" led by celebrities in many fields, Canadians joined together to contribute $27 million to Terry's vision. Canada had found a hero.

The story of humankind is liberally sprinkled with heroes. Growing up in Australia, I was fed a diet of heroes from British and Australian history. As I recall it, the earliest stories with which we were regaled by our teachers were those of Scott of the Antarctic, and the pioneer Australian pilot Sir Charles Kingsford-Smith, the war nurses Florence Nightingale and Edith

1

Cavell, explorers Edmund Kennedy and David Livingstone, and outstanding political figures such as Abraham Lincoln. This was toward the end of World War II, and our heroes were persons who gave themselves unstintingly in the service of their country—and were "faithful unto death"; or explorers in various fields who braved the unknown and died still pushing on—in the frigid wasteland near the South Pole (Scott), through the jungles of Africa (Livingstone) or North Australia (Kennedy), or flying solo from England to Australia (Kingsford-Smith). Soon for Australian boys there were other heroes on the horizon: cricketers and footballers, swimmers and runners and tennis players. And there were more from our wider history: Columbus and Cromwell, Washington and Wellington, Queen Elizabeth I and Queen Victoria, Shakespeare and Handel and Bach. There were some who were profoundly important for me, whose life stories I knew in intimate detail, who captured my imagination and deeply influenced my understanding of how life should be lived: Australia's all-time cricket great, Don Bradman; the British general of World War II, Montgomery of Alamain; John Wesley, riding up and down eighteenth-century England on horseback to preach the Christian message to the common folk; Albert Schweitzer, theologian and musician, leaving the comforts and fame of Europe to become a medical missionary in Africa; Mahatma Gandhi, walking through the villages of India in a nonviolent battle against the oppressions of an imperialist government.

Every culture has its saints and heroes—persons who capture our imagination by their actions or their teachings or both.

Founder Figures

A singularly important aspect of human religiousness in the last two thousand years or so has been the place of certain great heroes often referred to as "founder figures." If one compares the religious styles of the so-called great religions or world religions—religious communities that have spread across the globe and have held the allegiance of hundreds of millions of followers—with that of archaic or primitive societies, one cannot but be amazed at the extraordinary influence that the experiences of a handful of individuals have had on the life of the world.

This is not by any means to say that founder figures are unimportant for primitive or archaic societies. Almost universally in such societies there are stories of ancestors or gods who set the foundational structures of the society or of the world or of both. But the founding figures of the great religious traditions are different from those of archaic and primitive societies in a number of respects. The first is that each is related not just to a tribe or a state but to a community that reaches out across local and national boundaries. Moreover the religious communities often identify themselves quite closely with the founder figure—Buddhists as followers of the Buddha, Christians as those who have faith in Jesus the Christ, the "anointed one" of God. A second major difference is that, as we shall note more carefully later, in many respects they bear more resemblance to another figure found in many archaic and primitive societies—the warrior hero. There are numerous accounts of the hero who overcomes enemies, battles against powerful, dangerous forces in the world, and achieves great benefits for his people. The founders of the great traditions also perform such feats, but in a "spiritual" rather than a military context.

A third major difference of these religious founder figures from archaic founders is that, as with the warrior heroes, the achievements of the spiritual hero are quite specific. For primitive founders, the emphasis is upon the establishment of basic foundational structures of life; for the founders of the great religious traditions, interest is rather more focused on a particular theme or lifestyle. Almost all are pictured as offering or pointing the way to salvation or liberation of some kind. Frequently we have evidence of old patterns breaking down, and the unity of cosmos and culture seen in primitive and archaic cultures has been lost. In periods of uncertainty and fluidity the founders of the great religious traditions provided new lifestyles, each distinctive, each found by their followers to be satisfying and fulfilling.

One should be aware also that there were others who were important about the same time as the great founder figures, men whose movements rivaled for a time those that have survived. There was a time, for example, when the followers of Zarathustra, Mani, and Mahavira were quite numerous. That the way of Mani eventually proved less popular than that of Jesus may have been due to quite external circumstances of history; or to the influence of a Saint Augustine who became a Christian after a time as a Manichee, during which period he gradually became convinced that the way of Mani was not adequate to his own human quests and needs. Again, it may have been that the teaching of Mani was inherently less satisfying, less capable of providing persons with an appropriate vision of the world. The case of the Jains and the Buddhists is an interesting one in this regard. It has been remarked that the way of Mahavira, the leader of the Jains, is to that of the Buddha as is a somewhat clumsy earthen pot to a finely wrought vase (Eliot, I, 123). When one studies the Jains, one cannot but be fascinated by both their ideas and their actions; but, as this remark attests, one also is not really surprised that the Jain movement has remained relatively small.

In this work, I shall be looking at a number of figures whose movements have remained highly viable down to our own times—from India, Gautama the Buddha and Krishna; Kung-tzu and Lao-tzu in China; Moses and Jesus from among the Jews, and Muhammad from Arabia.

My inclusion of Krishna in this list—he fits quite naturally alongside the others—raises an important point. As I shall show in some detail later, Krishna was not "the founder of a religion." But that fact makes me wonder whether to talk in this way is adequate for any of these figures.[1] One might broaden the terminology a little and talk of them as *foundational* figures, for the life and teaching of each of them is in some sense a foundation upon which myriads of others have built their lives.

But other ways of thinking about these men are even more helpful. Thinking back to the array of heroes of my childhood, I am struck by the number of explorers who were included. And this category is most helpful for thinking about Gautama and Krishna and Jesus and Kung. More than that, they were discoverers, "breakthrough figures." In times when established views of the world and how life should be lived were beginning to be not fully satisfactory, each of these figures broke through to a new vision, saw things in a new way. They saw a light—and were able to shed light on the path of life in such a way that millions of others accepted their vision.

An important point here is that others were able to see what they saw; others were able to respond to their vision, found their teaching cogent and their lives sustaining. I like to think of each of the great religious traditions and communities of this world as a discovery shared, the transmission of a vision, the passing on of a lamp for the path of life.

The discovery by each of these breakthrough figures of a way that was experienced by their followers as sustaining and liberating led to a common phenomenon: frequently their followers have been highly evangelical. An offshoot of the conviction that they had good news to share with others has often—not always, but often—been a kind of exclusiveness. One can certainly see it in the Christian tradition. "God loved the world so much that he gave his only Son . . ." (John 3:16). Jesus said, "I am the way; I am the truth and I am life; no one comes to the Father except by me" (John 14:6). It has proved difficult for believers to say both that they have been led on the right path *and* that there may be other paths. Having seen the light, many have been unable to refrain from proclaiming everything else darkness; or, at best, a light whose usefulness has now been surpassed. Christians have traditionally varied from saying of others, "They are in error, we have the truth," through "They have the questions and we have the answers," to "They have part of the truth, but we can offer the whole truth, for Christ is the Truth." There have recently been trends away from this among some leading theologians.[2] But many persons live with a confusion of the kind that can be seen from a *Time* report on the Fourth Synod of Catholic Bishops held at the Vatican in September 1974:

> Pope Paul had stressed in his opening speech that evangelism was a permanent task of the church, that the Gospel must be preached to all, "to ensure that every tongue confesses that Christ is the only Lord and Saviour." Yet he also noted that even "non-Christian religions must no longer be regarded as rivals, but as a field of lively, respectful interest" [Oct. 28, 1974, 69].

There is clearly a failure of logic here. Pope Paul expressed in his second statement a conviction that Christians must be sensitive to and tolerant of other religions. There has been a growing concern that religious-minded persons take each other seriously, engage in dialogue, and accept each other, at least provisionally, as recipients of the truth in different forms. His first statement, however, remained in the old exclusivist framework that sees Christ as the only way. Pope Paul's theology, it would appear, did not keep pace with his personal sensitivity.

It seems to me that there is a great need for a theology that does justice to the power of the vision of the leading figures of all the great religious traditions. It is important that it allow the foundational figures to stand side by side, without the kind of last-minute shift that undercuts all positions except one. And it seems to me that if this theology is to be adequate to the situation of the global village in which we live, it will not be sufficient even to assert that Jesus and Gautama and Moses were "breakthrough figures" in the sense of offering a breakthrough to those of the community that looks to them for guidance. It will be necessary to be able to see them as each engaged in a breakthrough for us all. It is no longer adequate to assert that Buddhists have what is the truth for them, and Christians have what is the truth for them; we must at least explore the possibility that both the Christian and the Buddhist would be enriched by each other's vision. In fact, I am arguing in this work that there is no justification for the assumption made so often in the past that the visions of foundational leaders are mutually incompatible or contradictory. I shall attempt to show them as essentially complementary visions.

In doing this I believe we shall begin to move theologically in a direction that allows us to do greater justice to various historical movements. There has been considerable sharing across traditions—for example, among Christian, Jewish and Islamic theologians—to the extent that it is possible to assert with Wilfred Cantwell Smith that the Buddha is a Christian Saint,[3] with some Hindus that Jesus is an avatar of Vishnu (Akhilananda, 15–44), with some Buddhists that Jesus was a Buddhist. Such a theology will also, I hope, be more adequate to another phenomenon: when one thinks of such persons as Gandhi and Tagore, Schweitzer and Eliot and Yeats, for example, one is soon aware of the inadequacy in describing any of them as just Hindu or Christian. The experience and religious vision of each was far more complex than such simple nomenclature suggests. Each was quite profoundly affected by ideas deriving from a variety of traditions.

Not long ago I was asked to lead a seminar at a church convention—a seminar on meditation. Inevitably, discussion moved to a recent notable movement in North America, Transcendental Meditation (TM). I found myself suddenly embroiled in an argument about the legitimacy of TM for Christians. I was startled to discover that both sides in the dispute adhered to a position that I found quite untenable. One group argued that TM was all right because it was merely a technique, it had nothing to do with religion; if one meditated, that had nothing to do with Hinduism. The other group argued that TM *was* Hinduism and therefore highly dangerous. For both groups, if one had to acknowledge that TM was "Hindu," that automatically made it unacceptable for a Christian. I was disappointed that they were limited in their thinking to such categorization. It seemed to me that one could well argue the values or dangers of TM on other grounds, but to brand anything Hindu as bad just because it is Hindu is clearly to do an injustice to countless Hindus who have lived life in a Hindu context, as well as to so many Christians who have found that in seeing things via the Hindu tradition their own vision has been expanded and enriched. What worried me most was that Christians should so drastically cut themselves off from anything that was not able to be called "Christianity." We cannot afford to go into the future of the planet Earth with such a divisive vision.

It is on account of these concerns that I am attempting here to develop a position that does justice to the most influential figures of our religious history and allows us to share in the paths they have elucidated for us. The method I am using is to move to a theological position via the study of myth, and via an awareness of the common patterns that occur in myths from a wide range of cultures. More specifically, I am suggesting that we look at the stories of the lives of the founders of the great religious traditions as myths.

To suggest to Christians that they see the life of the Buddha as myth would probably worry them not at all. To suggest to Christians that they see the life of Jesus as myth would be profoundly disturbing to many. The reason is that in the culture at large, myths are generally taken to be untrue stories, with the implication that they are insignificant tales, appropriate in our enlightened age only as children's stories.

I am using the term "myth" in the context of recent scholarly studies—studies that take myths seriously, and do not by any means see them as insignificant. I also am not suggesting that the stories about these leaders are necessarily historically inaccurate. Rather, with Alan Watts, I am thinking of myths as "stories—some no doubt fact, and some fantasy—which, for various reasons, human beings regard as demonstrations of the inner meaning of the universe and of life" (Watts, 7). In suggesting that we see the stories of the Buddha and the stories of Jesus as myth, I mean that these stories offer profound insights into the meaning of life; and also that we may do well to bypass the question of historical accuracy.

From within the history of the Buddhist and Christian traditions there is good reason why we should do this. It is obvious that in the case of both Gautama "the Buddha" and Jesus "the Christ" the life stories that have come down to us have been mediated to us by particular interests of early Christians and early Buddhists, and rarely, it seems, were the primary interests of the story collectors historical. In addition, in each case the stories were set down some time after the death of the leader. In the case of the Buddha, it was some centuries before there was a written account; in the case of Jesus, probably thirty to forty years. The amount of time involved is not necessarily of crucial importance, because, as is well known, among a people where oral methods of transmission are primary, a piece of highly significant religious material can be passed on unchanged for centuries. India has offered scholars many demonstrations of such transmission.

Christians are often taken up with establishing the historical reliability of the Gospels, though whether they should be is another question. It is fairly clear that the gospel writers (with the possible exception of Luke),[4] in putting together their collections of stories, were not primarily interested in establishing beyond doubt that the stories as they told them were historically accurate. They were interested, rather, in presenting an important and exciting message, and they used their account of the life and teaching of Jesus as the vehicle for his message.

I am inclined to think that the historical reliability issue may be less important than scholars have made it.[5]

I should return here for a moment to an earlier point—that the vision of our great discoverers was equaled in importance by the fact that others found their vision compelling. In the case of all the traditions, what we have handed down to us is in the first instance the record of a response. The account of Jesus—or of the Buddha or of Master Kung—is a record of what his followers remembered as significant, a record of their own responses to the discovery, the vision, presented in the teaching and the living of their leader. And this is not necessarily a problem. For surely in the final analysis the validity of the Christian message depends upon the fact that Christians have found it true in their own experience.

Think for a moment about the story of the resurrection of Jesus from death. For an enormous number of Christians the historicity of this event is of crucial importance: they see it as establishing the uniqueness of Christianity—none of the other great leaders returned from the dead! Yet the idea of a body rising from death is beset with all kinds of difficulties for persons with a modern understanding of biological processes. In addition, when one tries to think of such a story from within an Indian context, one soon realizes that the significance of the story, taken literally, is quite local. In fact Hindus believe that we are all essentially eternal, and that is not triumph but a problem. To say, "because he lives, we too shall live—forever" is not so positive for them. Who would want to live forever?

One soon begins to realize that the idea of a risen body, the stories related to it, and the use made of these stories by Paul when he refers to a final resurrection of all at the last day, when "the trumpet shall sound," makes sense only in the context of Hebraic thought, where there was a strong resistance to the idea of survival beyond death as a merely spiritual thing. The Jews had such a strong sense that the full human individual is a complex of bodily and psychic and spiritual elements—the dust of the earth enlivened by the breath of God, one might say—that Greek ideas that the final human destiny is to be thought of in the survival of the soul were quite repugnant to them.

But although the event of the resurrection and its relationship to a final resurrection for all humanity are somewhat limited and limiting ideas, the implications that are drawn from this event are of much wider application. Others may find it difficult to comprehend the significance of a risen body, but few would be unable to enter the experience of the disciples in their realization that Jesus was not dead but living, that the kind of life he lived had such great significance that it transcended death. And similarly, because of numerous analogies in other cultures, few would be unable to comprehend the significance that Paul draws from the resurrection, when he relates the death-resurrection event to the experience of a person in baptism:

> Did you not die with Christ and pass beyond reach of the elemental spirits of the universe? Then why behave as though you were still living the life of the world? Why let people dictate to you: "Do not handle this, do not taste that, do not touch the other"—all of them things that must perish as soon as they are used? That is to follow merely human injunctions and teaching. True, it has an air of wisdom, with its forced piety, its self-mortification, and its severity to the body; but it is of no use at all as combating sensuality. Were you not raised to life with Christ? Then aspire to the realm above, where Christ is, seated at the right hand of God and let your thoughts dwell on that higher realm, not on this earthly life. I repeat, you died; and now your life lies hidden with Christ in God. . . . Then put to death those parts of you which belong to the earth. . . . Then put on the garments that suit God's chosen people, his own, his beloved: compassion, kindness, humility, gentleness, patience. Be forbearing with one another, and forgiving, where any of you has cause for complaint: you must forgive as the Lord forgave you. To crown all, there must be love, to bind all together and complete the whole [Col. 2:20–3:3, 3:5, 12–14].

The resurrection as an experience of renewal and enlivening power is something that has profound implications for all of us.

But such issues in relation to the life of Jesus we shall look at more fully later. It is sufficient at present to note that one of the great advantages of bypassing the question of historical accuracy is that it allows us to look at the stories of these breakthrough figures side by side. When we do this, we are able to observe some major similarities, which begin to make sense in the light of studies of myths. For it becomes clear that the life stories have a certain archetypal or universal quality about them, that they participate in a common vision of the spiritual hero. When we look more closely, however, we observe that there are also some differences. A careful examination of these differences suggests that particular emphases in the stories can be correlated with central aspects of the teaching of the leader concerned. The particular form of the story mediates important aspects of the message that the particular teacher has for the world.

Method and Order

My method of treatment of these figures needs some explication. In each case I have begun with ten sayings attributed to the teacher. My model for this was the Decalogue, the "ten words" or Ten Commandments given by God to Moses on Mount Sinai, the central core of Jewish teaching. I might well have decided to pick other numbers for other cultures where ten is not so significant a figure, but it seemed to be appropriate to try to encapsulate the teaching of each in somewhat similar fashion. So I stayed with ten. In each case I have used selections from what are accepted as the most basic, and generally the simplest, presentation of the given teaching. What I selected was determined by my conviction that there is a focus, a central core, to the teaching of each of these breakthrough figures. In subsequent discussion, in my attempt to explicate that core, I frequently make references to elements I have included in the ten sayings.

One will notice that the sayings of the different teachers are of vastly different styles. The ten injunctions of Moses are strong and sharp, the Analects of Kung are pithy aphorisms, the sayings from the *Dhammapada* are beautiful in their simple profundity. But others are more difficult. The teachings of Krishna in the *Bhagavad Gita* are presented in the form of an extended argument. In part, this is due to the fact that it derives from Indian sages, those who thought and spoke Sanskrit, who were guardians of the ancient intellectual heritage. Although I might have here also presented short selections, it seemed better to be more expansive in order to allow the discursive quality of the text to come through.

In the case of Jesus, the sayings are again short and sharp. But they are found within a context and it soon becomes clear that they disclose little of their meaning to us without the context. So the context is included.

I have begun, then, each exposition with these sayings. I might have concluded with them. Or I might suggest to readers that they return to them again at the end of the discussion. But I begin with them because they encapsulate the breakthrough, they are an invitation to discovery.

The order I have followed in discussing these great figures also merits some explanation. It is not chronological, nor is it strictly geographical. I begin with Gautama in India and end with Jesus, and in general there is a movement from East to West. But my beginning with the Buddha is determined somewhat by the fact that what I want to say in general about the life stories is done most easily by an initial comparison of Gautama and Jesus. In talking of Gautama I frequently assume some elementary knowledge of Jesus' life story. I am thus moving from known to unknown. But then in the light of the discussion I hope to enable us to see new dimensions in the familiar. Within the arena of India and the Far East it seemed most helpful to discuss Krishna and then Kung-tzu and Lao-tzu against the background already established by the discussion of Gautama.

That I have treated Moses and Muhammad together and Jesus last may seem an injustice to Muhammad: chronologically he comes last. Am I slighting Muhammad, keeping Jesus until last in yet another Christian imperialism—"last is best"? My reason for treating Moses and Muhammad together—I trust that I demonstrate this adequately—is that they go together. Their life stories, and also the vision of life that the stories reflect, are very similar.

That I treat Jesus after Moses and Muhammad is due to the fact that one cannot understand what Jesus is about except against the background of the discovery represented by Moses and Muhammad. That Muhammad came after Jesus, and that quickly what was a large part of the Christian world became Islamic, seems to me in part a critique of an inadequate understanding of the relation of Jesus to this background. When Christians kill each other because they have disagreements about how to set forth the significance of Jesus in philosophical language, something is wrong. The breakthrough of Jesus I find exciting and profound. But if it is broken off from its context in the vision given us by Moses and Muhammad it is dangerous and damaging. I have attempted to retain thoroughly that context.

I

CALM AS A LAKE: GAUTAMA, THE BUDDHA

TEN SAYINGS FROM THE *DHAMMAPADA*

We are what we think,
having become what we thought.
Like the wheel that follows the cart-pulling ox,
sorrow follows an evil thought.

And joy follows a pure thought
like a shadow faithfully tailing a man.
We are what we think
having become what we thought.

(Ten Twin Verses)

Like an archer an arrow,
the wise man steadies his trembling mind,
a fickle and restless weapon. . . .

The mind is restless.
To control it is good.
A disciplined mind is the road to Nirvana.

(Mind)

Who conquers this world,
*   the world of Yama and the world of the gods?*
Like a connoisseur picking a flower,
*   the good man chooses* Dhamma. . . .

Like floods that come and collect an unsuspecting village,
death claims the restless collector of flowers.

(Flowers)

"These sons are mine.
This wealth is mine."
The words of a fool.
He himself is not his.
How can sons be his?
How can wealth be his?

(The Fool)

Wind will not move rock,
nor praise and blame a wise man.
The words of the Dhamma *flow into him:*
he is clear and peaceful like a lake.

(The Wise Man)

No suffering for him
who is free from sorrow
free from the fetters of life
free in everything he does.
He has reached the end of his road.
He has no fixed habitation;
like a swan flown from its lake,
he is serious, he has left his home. . . .

He has found freedom—
peaceful his thinking, peaceful his speech,
peaceful his deed, tranquil his mind.

(The Saint)

All fear punishment, all fear death.
Therefore do not kill, or cause to kill.
Do as you would want done to you. . . .

Speak gently, and they will respond.
Angry words hurt, and rebound on the speaker. . . .

What matters if he dresses well?
If his mind is serene, chaste, firm,
if he practices nonviolence,
he is the Brahmin, the ascetic, the bhikku.

(Punishment)

The world is burning:
why is there laughter, why the sounds of joy?
Seek enlightenment, O fool,
for the darkness surrounds you.

Look at it—this painted shadow,
this body, crumbling, diseased, wounded,
held together by thoughts that come and go. . . .

Like glittering royal chariots slowly rusting,
the body moves into old age.
"Only virtue is stainless" is the only wisdom.

(Old Age)

Give up both pleasant and unpleasant!
Missing the pleasant is pain, and
finding the unpleasant is also pain.

To lose what one loves is pain.
For which reason, control the senses.
Only he is free who neither likes nor dislikes.

(Pleasure)

Craving is like a creeper,
it strangles the fool.
He bounds like a monkey, from one birth to another,
looking for fruit.

When craving, like poison,
takes hold of a man,
his sorrows increase
like wild grass.

(Craving)[6]

From Sensuality to Asceticism to Enlightenment

There are many accounts of the life of Gautama the Buddha. Some of them are quite late and are accepted by only a limited group of Buddhists. The story as it is accepted more or less universally among Buddhists is told in the *Buddhacarita* of Ashvaghosha, and in the introduction to the "Jataka" or birth narratives included in the *Tipitaka*, the "three baskets" of writings accepted as the scriptures by Theravada Buddhists.[7] Briefly the story runs as follows.

The evolution of the Buddha had gone on over an incalculable number of eons, through innumerable births.[8] Gradually he had risen in the scale of beings until it had become evident that he would one day become a Buddha. It was during the time of an earlier Buddha, Dipankara, that the present Buddha, then a king called Sumedha, vowed to become a Buddha.

The present phase of the story opens on a scene of the future Buddha dwelling in a heaven known as Tushita or "satisfied."[9] There is a proclamation by world messengers (more or less an equivalent of angels in Christian mythology)[10] that after a lapse of a thousand years a Buddha will arise in the world. When the gods (the deities of the Hindu pantheon are shared also by Buddhists) hear the message, they go and request the future Buddha to undergo the final stage of his evolution toward Buddhahood. After careful consideration of certain questions, such as whether the time was ripe, what would be the appropriate place in which to become a Buddha and who would be appropriate as the mother of a Buddha, the future Buddha undertakes a further birth onto the human stage, and is conceived by Queen Mahamaya, the wife of a king of the Shakya clan, which lived at that time in the eastern part of the valley of the Ganges. At the midsummer festival, the queen, in her fifty-fourth year, has a dream of a superb white elephant that circumambulates her couch three times, in an auspicious clockwise direction, strikes her on the right side, and appears to enter her womb. When sixty-four Brahmans or priests are called in to prepare a horoscope for the newly conceived child, they declare that the child will be a male, who will become either a universal monarch or a Buddha.

At the time of the conception of the future Buddha, all the ten thousand worlds trembled, and there were thirty-two marvelous signs:

> An immeasurable light spread through ten thousand worlds; the blind recovered their sight, as if from desire to see this his glory; the deaf received their hearing; the dumb talked; the hunchbacked became straight of body; the lame recovered the power to walk; all those in bonds were freed from their bonds and chains; the fires went out in all the hells; the hunger and thirst of the [ancestral dead] was stilled; wild animals lost their timidity; diseases ceased among men; all mortals became mild-spoken; horses neighed and elephants trumpeted in a manner sweet to the ear; all musical instruments gave forth their notes without being played upon; bracelets and other ornaments jingled; in all quarters of the heavens the weather became fair; . . . celestial music was heard to play in the sky; and the whole ten thousand worlds became one mass of garlands of the utmost possible magnificence [Warren, 44].

Toward the end of her pregnancy the mother of the future Buddha decided to go home to visit her relatives, and on the way she gave birth to her son in a pleasure garden called the Lumbini grove. She gave birth while standing upright, steadying herself by holding onto a branch of a *sal* tree. The child, when he came out from his mother's side feet first, was received by a golden net held by four angels.[11] Two streams of water fell from the heavens refreshing the child and his mother. Soon he took seven steps—he was followed by the god Brahma who held over him a white umbrella—and at the seventh, he shouted, "The chief am I in all the world." And because the womb that has borne a future Buddha is like a shrine in a temple, and thus could never rightly be occupied by another child or used in any other way, Queen Mahamaya died when he was seven days old.

Not long after, there was a visit from an ascetic who was a friend of the king. The ascetic, named Kaladevala in some versions and Asita in others, perceiving that the child would become a Buddha, wept; as he explains it, he weeps because, old as he is, he will not live to see the child after he has become a Buddha.

Later, there is a return of Brahman fortune-tellers who cannot agree in their interpretations of the child's horoscope.[12] The youngest one predicts that the child will be a Buddha, and indicates that what will cause the future Buddha to retire from the world will be a sight of an old man, a sick man, a dead man, and a *sannyasin*, "ascetic."

The father of the future Buddha, who preferred to see his son become a great king rather than a Buddha, tried to ensure that he not see anything of those troubling aspects of life—old age, sickness, death. He provided him with the most sumptuous luxuries possible, built him three palaces, and surrounded him with thousands of dancing girls. Gautama, as he was called, married a beautiful girl named Yashodhara, and proceeded to live a thoroughly sensual life. Although the king did everything to keep him from seeing the four signs, the gods intervened. When the future Buddha went one day for a ride in his chariot, although the king had all old persons removed from the vicinity of his journey, the gods created an old man. Upon the young prince, who had never seen such an aspect of life, the encounter had a profound effect. As Ashvaghosha says, "The prince reacted to this news like a bull when a lightning-flash crashes down near him" (Conze, 39). Subsequent similar encounters with sickness and death convince him that he must find a way of life consistent with these aspects of human existence. With the further vision of a *sannyasin*—a person who has given up ordinary life and its attachments to live an austere life in the forest—he also resolves to become an ascetic.

Just after this his son Rahula is born; the name is significant: it means "impediment." The future Buddha, however, will not let even so strong a temptation hold him back, and one night, after a glimpse of his sleeping wife and child, he leaves the palace secretly under cover of darkness, with the help of his trusted servant Channa and his horse Kanthaka. The tempter Mara tries to get him to return by promising him an enormous empire of four continents, but to no avail. After a journey of a hundred miles, Gautama, the future Buddha, takes off his ornaments, and cuts off the hair of his topknot, the tuft of uncut hair worn by men of the Indian upper classes. The hair is received by the god Indra in an appropriate jeweled casket.

Now begins a life of harsh austerities, in which he lives on one grain of rice or one sesame seed per day. The effect of this treatment was that his body became emaciated, and burned black, losing its characteristic golden hue. He spent six years like this. At the end of that time he decided that it was time spent "endeavoring to tie the air in knots." He decided that if the sensual life he had lived had no fulfillment in it when viewed in the light of the old age, disease, and death that afflict the body, neither was there any final satisfaction in an obsessively harsh treatment of the body. He begs for food and begins to eat normally again.

The final stage of his progress toward the attainment of "enlightenment" has now arrived. There is a story of his being fed by a young woman, called Sujata in the "Jakatas," Nandabala in the *Buddhacarita*. After eating forty-nine balls of food, he does not eat again for forty-nine days, or seven weeks. Having eaten he goes and sits under a large tree, the Bo tree as it is called (meaning "the tree of enlightenment"), on the eastern side, facing west, and he begins to meditate. As he sits there, the tempter Mara makes his last concerted attack to try to stop him from becoming a Buddha. Mara sends storms of wind, rain, rocks, weapons, live coals, hot ashes, sand, mud, darkness, hoping to divert him from his goal, but all these attacks are unsuccessful. Mara hurls his discus, but it is changed into a canopy of flowers. The daughters of Mara appear before Gautama and try to tempt him with their sensual dances, but to no avail. Finally, after he has called upon the earth to witness to his acts of generosity over many years— which the earth does with thunderous roars—the army of Mara flees, and the gods proclaim the victory of Prince Siddhartha.[13] Throughout the night, he continues in meditation, entering into deeper and deeper knowledge or wisdom, finally becoming enlightened.

About the nature of this enlightenment the texts have little to say. As at the time of his conception, there is a picture of the universe responding empathetically in joy at the attainment of enlightenment. And again, "the blind from birth received their sight; the deaf from birth their hearing; the cripples from birth the use of their limbs; and the bonds and fetters of captives broke and fell off" (Warren, 83).

For seven days he sat there. Then, being tempted at first not to share what he had discovered—Mara returns to try to prevent this great vision from being shared among humanity—he was prevailed upon by Indra and Brahma, the chief gods, and thereupon set out to free the world.

The first persons to whom he preached were five holy men who had been his friends when he had been an ascetic. They had been disgusted with him for giving up the ascetic path, but when he approached them they found themselves inadvertently acknowledging him as their teacher. He taught them of the middle way, the noble eightfold path, and the four noble truths (Conze, 56).

The rest of the story is made up of various accounts of conversions, pictures of the daily life of the Buddha and his close disciples. His father visits him and acknowledges his greatness. His cousin Devadatta figures in a number of stories. He corresponds somewhat to Judas in the story of Jesus, for he is the enemy within the ranks of the disciples, and is continually portrayed as trying to destroy the Buddha's work. Finally, there is the account of the death of the Buddha at the age of eighty. Scholars are undecided whether it was pork or mushrooms that caused his death, but he appears to have died from some variety of food poisoning.

Parallels with the Life of Jesus

A comparison of this story with the popular accounts of the life of Jesus reveals some interesting parallels. In both cases there is what could be described as a miraculous conception. In both cases the conception and birth are given a cosmic setting, with superhuman beings in attendance. In both cases, the presence of this person on the mundane stage is good news for the blind, the deaf, the lame, those in bondage. Both lives are clearly seen as of profound importance for the human condition with all its pains and sadness and terrors.

The journey of Mahamaya to visit her kinsfolk reminds one of Mary's visit to her cousin Elizabeth. The parallel is even closer to the story of the birth of Jesus preserved in Islamic tradition, in which Mary gives birth beneath a palm tree (see below, p. 115). The death of Queen Mahamaya and the tradition that Mary is ever virgin serve similar functions, in that both are clearly an attempt to ensure the purity of the vessel that bears this perfect one.

Representatives of the old traditions also serve similar functions. The Hindu sage Asita and the Jewish wise man Simeon each witness to their vision of the greatness of the child. Their responses are two sides of a coin. Asita weeps because he will not live to see the child become the Buddha, the enlightened one; Simeon praises God because, although he will not live to see the mature life of the Messiah, he has seen the salvation of the Lord in its beginnings. The difference is quite significant, for their words correspond to different emphases within the Buddhist and Christian traditions; for Buddhists the experience of enlightenment is central to the life of the Buddha and to the Buddhist path. For Christian theologians the idea of the incarnation has often been seen as the central clue to understanding the life of Jesus and the experience of the Christian—that is, Christian theologians have frequently seen what happens in the cross of Jesus as already begun in his birth.

As well as these sensitive sage figures, both stories also include more formal representatives of the old traditions. The Brahman astrologers, and the priests in Jerusalem who are to tell where the Messiah is to be born by consulting the ancient prophecies, appear as those who know but do not know. They are able to give the formal answers, but do not have the vision to go further.

A very important similarity is the retreat into the wilderness that precedes the ministry of each. The stimulus for setting off is quite different: Gautama sets off in order to find the answer to certain pressing problems of human existence, and as a result of his wilderness experience he finds the answer, he becomes enlightened. Jesus, on the other hand, is pictured as to some extent aware already that he constitutes the answer, and the time in the wilderness involves a wrestling with its implications. But in both cases the focus of the wilderness experience is a battle with hostile forces, and it climaxes in the victory over the evil one.

Finally there is the ministry of teaching and healing. In the case of the Buddha there is little healing recorded; despite the motif of the healing of blind, deaf, dumb, deformed, and lame in the poetic presentation of the effects of the conception of the future Buddha, the Buddha himself was concerned with a different kind of transformation of human life—one that would enable humankind to live with the painfulness of human experience. Thus, according to one story, when a woman whose son had just died came to him begging him to restore her son to life, the Buddha sent her around the houses of her village to see if she could find a home that death had not touched. If she could, he said, he would restore her son to life. But the woman found that there was indeed no one exempt from the painfulness of the loss of a loved one. And clearly the Buddha's message is expressly designed to take seriously the fact of death.

The Hero in Ancient Myth

That there are so many similarities between the lives of these two great figures requires some explanation. A possible explanation is the drift of stories across the world, presumably from India to the area around the eastern Mediterranean where the stories about the life of Jesus developed. The implication of this would be that those recounting the life of Jesus borrowed stories from the life of the Buddha to elucidate their picture of Jesus.[14] Although this is certainly possible, for we know that there were many contacts between the two cultures around this time, there is no evidence in other literature from the Hellenistic period of a strong interest in the life or teaching of the Buddha.[15]

A more fruitful way of looking at these similarities is to be seen in the writings of Joseph Campbell, particularly in his book *The Hero with a Thousand Faces*. From an examination of numerous stories of heroes from many different cultures, Campbell puts together a composite picture of the story of the hero. He presents it in briefest outline:

> The mythological hero, setting forth from his commonday hut or castle, is lured, carried away, or else voluntarily proceeds, to the threshold of adventure. There he encounters a shadow presence that guards the passage. The hero may defeat or conciliate this power and go alive into the kingdom of the dark (brother-battle, dragon-battle; offering, charm), or be slain by the opponent and descend in death (dismemberment, crucifixion). Beyond the threshold, then, the hero journeys through a world of unfamiliar yet strangely intimate forces, some of which severely threaten him (tests), some of which give magical aid (helpers). When

he arrives at the nadir of the mythological round, he under-
goes a supreme ordeal and gains his reward. The triumph
may be represented as the hero's sexual union with the
goddess-mother of the world (sacred marriage), his recogni-
tion by the father-creator (father atonement), his own
divinization (apotheosis), or again—if the powers have remained unfriendly to him—his theft of the boon he came to
gain (bride-theft, fire-theft); intrinsically it is an expansion
of consciousness and therewith of being (illumination,
transfiguration, freedom). The final work is that of the return. If the powers have blessed the hero, he now sets forth
under their protection (emissary); if not, he flees and is pursued (transformation flight, obstacle flight). At the return
threshold, the transcendental powers must remain behind;
the hero reemerges from the kingdom of dread (return, resurrection). The boon that he brings restores the world
(elixir) [Campbell, 245–46].

Campbell points out that this pattern in which a call to adventure results eventually in a moment of discovery and leads finally
to the return to ordinary life of a person profoundly "regrouped"
or renewed as a result of the discovery experience is also the pattern for initiation in numerous cultures. We can see that it also
explains the appeal of religious retreats, vacations, and the "human potential" movement.

In terms of hero stories themselves, it seems to me that there are
basically two different kinds of stories told about ancient heroes:
one is a battle against alien powers—powers of evil, darkness,
chaos, perhaps drawing upon the experience of early human communities surrounded by wilds in which often dwelt marauding
animals that terrorized the small communities. One who was able
to establish peace and order for the community by ridding it of the
dangerous and threatening forces would naturally draw a deep
response from his fellows.[16] The other major hero story is that of a
journey in quest of something valuable—jewels, pearls, a
treasure, the Golden Fleece, a plant or font of immortality.[17] The
different forms mentioned here make it clear how easily one can
drift in these stories from the quest for something mundane, the
glories of gold and glittering jewels, to the quest for an essence of

that transcendent quality of human experience of which humans have been aware now for at least some four thousand years.[18]

These two different kinds of stories are most succinctly referred to as "test" and "quest" stories. Although they often occur quite independently, it is also not uncommon for the quest story to include within it a test story—presumably from the awareness that the most precious aspects of human experience are not arrived at without a struggle. Again the combined motif can be applied equally to mundane pursuits and to the quest for something more "spiritual," more ultimate, more qualitatively "real." Campbell has drawn the two motifs together in such a way that the composite fits most of our great religious figures. It fits well both Gautama and Jesus.

Campbell also notes that a common motif for the hero is the way his life is given cosmic scope, the way the great significance of this leader for his followers is expressed. Very common are two themes we have seen in relation to Gautama and Jesus—the miraculous birth and the setting of deities and angels, the great powers of the world, who witness to or, one might say, resonate with the stupendous importance of what is taking place (see Campbell, 311–33).

Buddhist and Christian Comparisons

Having been awakened by Campbell to this widespread motif of the hero's quest, one can go further and observe that the distinctive way in which this heroic pattern is treated tells us a great deal about the central message that the life of a particular hero is meant to convey. If one thinks comparatively about how much time is taken in the accepted stories of Gautama and Jesus by this cycle of adventure, one cannot but be astounded by the difference. In the case of Jesus, the cycle takes but a few verses; in the case of Gautama it is the larger part of the story of his life. It encompasses the central events of the great renunciation and the long road through asceticism to the battle against the hosts of Mara and finally the awakening, the enlightenment. The point of this great emphasis is to be seen, I think, in the fact that this central part of the life of Gautama is a portrayal in story form of the Buddhist message (see above, p. 21).

We can come to see this only if we look at some of the most basic presentations of the Buddhist message. In order to do this, it is most helpful to look at three variant presentations of it. Two of these—the Four Noble Truths and the Three Signs of Existence— will be explored in some detail. The third, some sayings from the *Dhammapada*, I have used to begin this chapter; I shall be using some of these sayings to elucidate the other two presentations.

The Four Noble Truths are as follows: the first is the fact of suffering; the second is that suffering is due to desire or grasping; the third is that the way to the eradication of suffering is by means of the eradication of craving; the fourth is that the way to do this is to follow the noble eightfold path.

These statements tell one very little. They are rather in the nature of mnemonics, memory aids to facilitate the learning of the lesson of truth. Or they are like a skeleton upon which the flesh of the teaching can hang. They need, therefore, some exploration.

The first truth is that life is suffering: *duhkha* (Sanskrit), *dukkha* (Pali). The first thing to observe in an attempt to understand this statement is that non-Buddhists who have traveled much in Buddhist countries have not noted Buddhists as particularly sad persons. One needs to be reminded that suffering is not the whole picture, not the end of the story. The Buddhist teaching appears at first glance, in its focus on the painfulness of experience, as a rather pessimistic comment on human life. But by the time one has reached the end of the road, the end of the Buddhist path, one cannot but be amazed at the optimism of the Buddha. Further insight into what is meant by *duhkha* can be given if we are aware that it is the antonym to another word, *sukha*. "*Su-*" means "well," "good." "How are you?" we ask a friend. "Fine, thanks." *Duhkha* is an assertion of what we may well know if we know the friend well: that "fine" is too onesided, too superficial. Life, say the Buddhists, is "*duh*," which might be thought of as an equivalent of "ugh!" "Life is a drag!" must be added to the perception of life as fine. *Su* and *duh*, pleasure and pain, go hand in hand.

This focusing on the negative side of human experience is designed to take one beyond a superficial optimism. Any valid approach to life has to take into consideration pain and death.

It is interesting to observe that for Christians too suffering is a

central fact of human experience. The very different approaches
to the fact of suffering in the case of Christians and Buddhists
might be seen in comparing a picture of Christ on the Cross (for
example, the Eisenheim altarpiece of Matthias Grünewald) and a
sculpture of the Buddha sitting in meditation. The circumstances
of the painting of the Eisenheim altarpiece are illuminating:

> The hermits of St. Anthony in the Vosges in the fifteenth
> century . . . had to care for the victims of plague, typhus,
> bubonic plague and the terrible disease known as St. An-
> thony's fire—where the circulation stops and the lower
> limbs become gangrenous, stinking and putrefying even in
> life. There was little the hermits could do for such but pre-
> pare their patients for a terrible death. And then Matthias
> Grünewald came among them and painted that terrific pic-
> ture of Christ which is now in the museum at Colmar—a
> Christ dead, twisted, and repulsive, grey and green with
> corruption—his legs swollen as though with St. Anthony's
> fire—against a black sky and a Dead Sea.
> The hermits used to leave each new patient alone on his
> pallet before that picture—and most of them too ill to make
> anything of it—but now and then such a man would say—
> "In a few hours now I must go to my death through foul and
> meaningless pain. But so did He, and God turned that for
> Him to the salvation of mankind" [Rupp, 37–38].

Christians have often asserted that one cannot understand suffering; but in the light of the suffering of Jesus, they have also
asserted that one can find God in the midst of suffering. Some
have even suggested that one can find suffering at the heart of
God.

The images of the Buddha present a different picture. Here is
one who sits, the picture of perfect calm. His eyes, closed or half
closed in meditation, are transparent with lucidity, and the clear
vision is attended by the flicker of a smile on the Buddha's lips.
And the inner peace exudes to the surface of the skin, so that the
stone surface discloses to us, in an incredible portrayal of smooth-
ness and fluidity, this person who is completely without the agita-
tion and straining that is evidenced in tension knots and bulging
muscles.

Thus, one might say that whereas the Christian message has involved a transformation of suffering by an immersion into it, the Buddhist message has involved a transcendence of it, and a transformation of it, in the experience of meditation. But that must not divert us from the fact that the experience of suffering is the initial fact, the backdrop against which the Buddhist message is played out.

Some of us may doubt that life is painful. Many of us living in the technological society of the latter half of twentieth century can easily bypass the painfulness of human existence. For us, the drudgery that characterized so many lives in past centuries is not something with which we have to contend. The suddenness of disease and death, striking out of nowhere, has been greatly reduced by the discoveries of medical science. Yet some commentators on the human condition are convinced that this may not be altogether a blessing. It may be that we can now too easily close our eyes to sickness and old age and death—to the extent that our lives are lived largely as though they are not part of our experience. Almost all our cultural heroes are beautifully or handsomely youthful. We find it so difficult to think of aged beauty that many of us spend enormous amounts of money and time trying to retain or regain a youthful appearance—with often ludicrous results. In addition, it has been observed, we place our sick, our deformed, and our tormented in institutions that effectively conceal from our view these reminders of more troublesome aspects of human life. And perhaps our biggest attempt to cloak the painful facts of life and death is to be seen in funeral homes where bodies are concealed beneath a cosmetic of life; or in Forest Lawn, Los Angeles, where a body can, for an appropriate fee, be arranged in such a way that it sits facing a beautiful scene of lawns and trees and flowers.[19]

Whatever we may say about our present condition, one thing is clear: the Buddhist approach begins with, is predicated upon, the fact that life is painful.[20] The next step toward appreciating the Buddhist message is to understand what is said in the next "truth"—that suffering is due to desire, craving, grasping. Initially we can think of this most easily if we think in terms of the frustration of desire. If we crave for something, the frustration of the fulfillment of our craving is painful. In the whirl of our grasping we long for something and we feel very unhappy if we do not get what we want; we have our selfish desires, and we get annoyed with someone who frustrates them.

A central clue in understanding this analysis of the relationship between desire and pain is in the Buddha's use of the image of fire:

> The world is burning:
> why is there laughter, why the sounds of joy?

Thus the *Dhammapada*. There is a much fuller presentation in the Buddha's Fire Sermon:

> All things, O monks, are on fire. And what, O monks, are all these things which are on fire?
>
> The eye, O monks, is on fire; forms are on fire; eye-consciousness is on fire; impressions received by the eye are on fire; and whatever sensation, pleasant, unpleasant, or indifferent, originates in dependence on impressions received by the eye, that also is on fire.
>
> And with what are these on fire?
>
> With the fire of passion, say I, with the fire of hatred, with the fire of infatuation; with birth, old age, death, sorrow, lamentation, misery, grief, and despair are they on fire.
>
> The ear is on fire; sounds are on fire; . . . the nose is on fire; odors are on fire; . . . the tongue is on fire; tastes are on fire; . . . the body is on fire; things tangible are on fire; . . . the mind is on fire; ideas are on fire; . . . mind-consciousness is on fire; impressions received by the mind are on fire; and whatever sensation, pleasant, unpleasant, or indifferent, originates in dependence on impressions received by the mind, that also is on fire.
>
> And with what are these on fire?
>
> With the fire of passion, say I, with the fire of hatred, with the fire of infatuation; with birth, old age, death, sorrow, lamentation, misery, grief, and despair are they on fire [Warren, 352].

We can understand this fairly easily. We know about "burning with desire." In the film *M*A*S*H* we met Hot Lips; and about the same time women were wearing "hot pants." In both cases the image of heat was being used as an image of desire, of intensity. But it is no great step from burning with desire to burning with the pain of unfulfilled craving; and it is this nuance that the Buddha was able to utilize so effectively.

One begins to see that a different way of thinking about painfulness is implied in this imagery. The primary focus is not physical pain; the pain of a toothache hardly seems relatable to desire or craving in the manner suggested here. The primary focus seems more emotional or, more broadly, in the area of the mind. The suggested is that the painfulness of existence is essentially a supraphysical thing.

In two verses from the *Dhammapada* the relationship between craving and pain or sorrow is explored in three further images. Craving is like a creeping vine that strangles a person; it is like poison; it makes one like a monkey looking for fruit—one bounds from one birth to another. The first two images we can understand fairly easily—craving can consume, poison, a person. The third takes us into another way of thinking than is customary in the West, that of transmigration or, as it is usually called in Buddhist writings, rebirth.

Much thinking of Indians around the time of the Buddha gave attention to the conviction that beings are reborn over and over again in different bodily forms; a widely accepted position was that the conditions of life into which one is born are the result of one's goodness or lack of it in one's previous life or lives. Gradually there develops a very negative view toward being reborn over and over again—the painfulness of existence becomes focused in this image of rebirth—and the goal of the religious path becomes for many, "not to return," freedom from rebirth. In the *Dhammapada*, then, the image of the monkey hopping restlessly from tree to tree in order to satisfy its craving for fruit is used as an image of the person impelled by craving and attachment to further births. But the image can reverse the process of explanation. The belief in rebirth is most easily understandable to us as a way of showing how human beings are trapped in the restlessness of their persistent cravings.

The aim of the Buddhist path, it thus becomes clear, is to enable persons to be released from the burning, the strangling, the poisoning, the persistent restlessness of their cravings and desires. Released from craving, one is released from pain.

A most important word needs to be introduced at this point, although it is not used in the Four Noble Truths. It is the word "nirvana" (*nirvāṇa*, Sanskrit; *nibbana*, Pali). It literally means "a blowing out." An important question that has frequently been asked is, "Of what is nirvana a blowing out?" Some have interpreted it as a blowing out of life entirely, and have seen it as a very negative path that the Buddha is presenting. Within the context of Buddhist thought, however, this seems to be a massive misunderstanding of what the Buddha is about. Nirvana seems rather to mean a blowing out, an eradication, of *desire* or craving. What that implies in positive terms is difficult to say. Perhaps one should say, more radically, that it is impossible to say, for it is impossible to describe nirvana. All description comes from the context of existence, which partakes centrally of painfulness; nirvana is somehow beyond existence. As the Buddha said, "There is an unborn, an unbecome, an unmade, an uncompounded; if there were not, how could there be release from the born, become, made, compounded?" (James, 85).

Insofar as Buddhists have tried to describe what is recognized as indescribable, they have used terms such as peace, or bliss (the highest happiness, beyond pleasure and pain, beyond even happiness and sorrow as we experience normal mundane experience) or, as I have already indicated, they have sculpted representations of the Buddha that portray in stone a peace that cannot be described in words.

But again a central image is that of fire: the one who has realized nirvana, the true saint, is like a fire that has been extinguished. The fire of desire is gone. The fire of pain is gone. The saint is one who has "cooled."

The path prescribed for the reaching of this goal is that of the Noble Eightfold Path, often called the Middle Way. The eight steps of the path are right views, right aspiration or intention, right speech, right conduct or action, right livelihood, right effort, right mindfulness, right meditation. These are presented not in a chronological sequence but in a psychological sequence. All must be followed continually. The sequence indicates the importance of the three aspects: initially, a correct focus or direction;

beyond that, appropriate conduct; and built upon the foundation of a good moral life, the practice of meditation.

The Buddhist moral code is remarkably like that found in other religions we shall look at: it includes such injunctions as the avoidance of untruth, killing, stealing, sexual immorality. There are further injunctions for monks. It soon becomes evident that the early Buddhists saw the path at its highest as open only to one who lives a celibate life and whose only worldly possessions are a begging bowl, a razor, a needle, a water-strainer, three robes, and a girdle.

It is surprising to us to hear this described as the middle path; to us it seems rather extreme. But to the Buddhist, what is indicated here is a path midway between harsh asceticism and debauchery. The result is a way that is finely honed, disciplined, directed toward the eradication—or perhaps we should say again, transcendence—of suffering. On this view, the way of debauchery is the fruitless attempt to avoid pain, and the way of asceticism is an equally fruitless attempt to escape pain through an overload of pain. The Buddhist way, one might suggest, renders craving ineffectual and pain irrelevant.

A more substantive understanding of how this path works—and the Buddhist way is intensely practical—is given by a consideration of the Three Signs of Existence—*duhkha, anitya* (Sanskrit; *anicca*, Pali), and *anatman* (Sanskrit; *anatta*, Pali). The Four Noble Truths are worked out in the context of *duhkha*. The three signs are best understood as variations on a theme. That is, one might also see the Three Signs of Existence as an assertion that the backdrop is *duhkha*; but further light is thrown on the nature of *duhkha* by consideration of *anitya* and *anatman*. These explanatory words, however, are not merely variations; they provide additional, and central, clues to the nature of the Buddhist path.

Anitya means "impermanence." Everything is constantly changing. If Heraclitus could say that you cannot step into the same river twice, the Buddhists know that you cannot step into the same river once, for it is changing even as you are stepping. And the misery, the painfulness, is in this, that everything passes away.

That all is transience is something that others besides Buddhists have realized. Christians sing a hymn in which there is the verse:

> Time like an ever-rolling stream
> Bears all its sons away.
> They fly forgotten, as a dream
> Dies at the opening day.[21]

The implication is clear in much Christian thinking: one should not cling to the things of this world. Do not put your trust in money; tomorrow there may be a crash of the stock market and, if there is nothing more abiding than money in your life, your state will be a sorry one. The same applies to food and drink and political achievements.

Christians have often made a distinction between grosser material things that cannot give full or abiding satisfaction and higher "spiritual" things that are more worthwhile—friendship, the joys of family, music, art. Buddhists are much more thoroughgoing in their perception of the fact of transience. Everything passes away—including friends, including sons and daughters. In the vision of radical impermanence, for parents to try to fulfill themselves in their children is as problematic as trying to find fulfillment in money or a fine house or a kingdom with all its showy magnificence.

The *Dhammapada* shows us another side of transience. If the outer world is characterized by transience, the inner world of the mind is characterized by restlessness, fickleness. Wise persons steady their mind. If one is caught up with the transient world, one is doomed to be a restless collector of flowers, one is condemned to being torn apart, distracted in the continued search for yet another fleeting moment of fulfillment.

Wise persons steady their mind. As a result they will be able to see transience for what it is. With clarity they will be able to see that there is nothing to cling to, that clinging means pain.

The full radicalness of the Buddhist position is evident only when we see the implications of *anatman,* the "no self" idea. An effective link between *anitya* and *anatman* is highlighted in a verse from the *Dhammapada:*

"These sons are mine.
This wealth is mine."
The words of a fool.
He himself is not his.
How can sons be his?
How can wealth be his?

If the Buddha is saying that one cannot find fulfillment in wealth or in sons—that clinging to them is no match for the all-pervasive pain of existence—he is also going further to say that one cannot find fulfillment in oneself. For there *is* no self.

This teaching is related to that of the great classical Hindu texts called the Upanishads.[22] Here there is a similar perception that the things of the world do not abide. In their seeking for what is permanent the upanishadic sages eventually came to use the term "Atman," the self, the permanent entity behind the shifting flux of our experience. As the upanishadic thinkers analyzed the human individual they became convinced that the body is not the self, the mind is not the self, the emotions are not the self. The self is beyond all that changes.

The Buddha asserted that there is no self. There *is* no permanent entity that abides. There is nothing, absolutely nothing, to which one can cling. "I" is merely a word, a practical designation. A person is no more than shifting flux.

It is arguable that the Buddha was not really saying anything different from the upanishadic writers. Christians have at times analyzed the central human problem (what Christians call sin) as self-centeredness or egocentricity, and both Buddhists and Hindus were able to see the problem in similar terms.[23] If the central cause of painfulness is clinging to what is transient, the most potent focus for clinging is the ego, one's individuality. The celebrated assertion in the Upanishad, "That art Thou"[24]—that ultimately the true self of the individual and the Self of the universe are one and the same—leads away from the narrowness of egocentricity.

Yet if one is left with a self that is permanent—even if it is the cosmic Self—there is still something to which to cling. And in his radical portrayal of nonclinging the Buddha takes what Hindus and Christians have understood in psychological terms and pushes it to its metaphysical limits. Beyond this shifting experience that I call myself there is nothing to which I can cling.

This raises a number of questions. One is: What, then, is reborn? The Buddhist answer is that in the process of continued rebirth, what happens is that a certain set of entities forms a conglomerate perceived as an individual. At death there is a dissolution of these elements. In accord with the karmic force, the weight of goodness that an individual has acquired, there is a regrouping of entities or elements to form a new conglomerate. But there is nothing that abides as the eternal link of all moments of conglomeration.

Is the Buddha a Nihilist?

This is a question we have asked before; it now returns in a more radical form. Is nirvana a blowing out of existence, a mere dissolution into nonexistence?

Put in the form in which this was asked of the Buddha, we may ask, "Does the one who has reached nirvana, the saint, cease to exist after death?" The answer of the Buddha as it has been recorded was as follows:

> "How is it, Gotama? Does Gotama hold that the saint exists after death, . . .?
>
> "How is it, Gotama? Does Gotama hold that the saint both exists and does not exist after death, and that this view alone is true, and every other false?"
>
> "Nay, Vaccha. I do not hold that the saint both exists and does not exist after death, and that this view alone is true, and every other false."
>
> "But how is it, Gotama? Does Gotama hold that the saint neither exists nor does not exist after death, and this view alone is true, and every other false?"
>
> "Nay, Vaccha. I do not hold that the saint neither exists nor does not exist after death, and that this view alone is true, and every other false. . . .
>
> "Vaccha, the theory that the saint neither exists nor does not exist after death is a jungle, a wilderness, a puppet-

show, a writhing, and a fetter, and is coupled with misery, ruin, despair, and agony, and does not tend to aversion, absence of passion, cessation, quiescence, knowledge, supreme wisdom, and *nirvana.*

"This is the objection I perceive to these theories, so that I have not adopted any one of them."

"But has Gotama any theory of his own?"

"The Tathagata, O Vaccha, is free from all theories but this, Vaccha, does the Tathagata know—the nature of form, and how form arises, and how form perishes; the nature of sensation, and how sensation arises, and how sensation perishes; the nature of perception, and how perception arises, and how perception perishes; the nature of the predispositions, and how predispositions arise, and how the predispositions perish; the nature of consciousness, and how consciousness arises, and how consciousness perishes. Therefore say I that the Tathagata has attained deliverance and is free from attachment, inasmuch as all imaginings, or agitations, or false notions concerning an ego or anything pertaining to an ego have perished, have faded away, have ceased, have been given up and relinquished."

"But, Gotama, where is the monk reborn who has attained to this deliverance for his mind?"

"Vaccha, to say that he is reborn would not fit the case."

"Then, Gotama, he is not reborn."

"Vaccha, to say that he is not reborn would not fit the case."

"Then, Gotama, he is both reborn and is not reborn."

"Vaccha, to say that he is both reborn and not reborn would not fit the case."

"Then, Gotama, he is neither reborn nor not reborn."

"Vaccha, to say that he is neither reborn nor not reborn would not fit the case. . . ."

"Gotama, I am at a loss what to think in this matter. . . ."

"But, Vaccha, if the fire in front of you were to become extinct, would you be aware that the fire in front of you had become extinct?"

"Gotama, if the fire in front of me were to become extinct, I should be aware that the fire in front of me had become extinct."

"But, Vaccha, if some one were to ask you, 'In which direction has that fire gone—east, or west, or north, or south?' what would you say, O Vaccha?"

"The question would not fit the case, Gotama. For the fire which depended on fuel of grass and wood, when that fuel has all gone, and it can get no other, being thus without nutriment, is said to be extinct."

"In exactly the same way, Vaccha, all form by which one could predicate the existence of the saint, all that form has been abandoned, uprooted, pulled out of the ground like a palmyra-tree, and become non-existent and not liable to spring up again in the future. The saint, O Vaccha, who has been released from what is styled form, is deep, immeasurable, unfathomable, like the mighty ocean. To say that he is reborn would not fit the case. To say that he is not reborn would not fit the case. To say that he is neither reborn nor not reborn would not fit the case" [Radhakrishnan and Moore, 289–91].

The point seems to be that the Buddha realizes that there are many questions that just cannot be answered. To attempt to answer them is a waste of time, fruitless. The questions are inappropriate to the human situation. On one occasion when the Buddha was asked questions like this, he said that to consider such questions was like coming across a man who has been shot with an arrow and is dying from loss of blood, and asking questions like, "Who shot the arrow? From what direction did it come? What was its trajectory? What are the materials that comprise the arrow, shaft and head?"—all questions irrelevant to the pressing need of the man who has been shot. What is needed is for someone to remove the arrow as quickly as possible and staunch the flow of blood. It is a matter of life and death calling for appropriate action.

The Buddha's path is a practical path to peace. Questions about life, beyond what can be examined and analyzed, are irrelevant. But the Buddha is certainly *not* nihilistic. He is one who has come through to a profound vision of how life should be lived. He has been awakened, woken up—that is what the word "buddha" means—to what life is about and what kind of living is appropriate. And what he woke up to, the kind of living that is appropriate, is at heart a profound realization of the flow of life—profound partly in the sense that one realizes it only with long periods of meditation—and a resultant simple life lived unclingingly, lived with lucidity.

The central part of the life story of Gautama fits this picture. The quest and test motifs are imbued with the central elements of the Buddhist message. What stimulates the quest is portrayed with some psychological finesse by way of the traditional belief that he was prevented from encountering sickness and old age and death. The conviction, common among the young, that they are invulnerable,[25] is here given an extreme form by virtue of the fact that the young Prince Gautama is not even theoretically aware of pain and death. As a result, the midlife crisis, when it comes in a sudden confrontation with the negative elements of existence, hits him much more powerfully than it does the rest of us. It provides a very powerful incentive toward finding a life appropriate to the facts of both pleasure and pain. And because the confrontation has been so shattering, the quest is correspondingly profound. Easy answers, unsatisfactory paths, will not suffice. Winning through, breaking through, to the goal, involves a long quest and many battles against adverse forces, forces that will tempt him to be satisfied with a superficial answer. The psychological conditions are appropriate to one who is to become a Buddha, to one who achieves a heroic breakthrough in showing others how to find peace.

The extensive treatment of the quest motif is also important for what it teaches about the Buddhist way. With their psychological awareness, the Buddhists know that the finding of this profound peace is not easy. It entails a long, careful, and disciplined trek.

When preachers of my childhood waxed eloquent, they told a sentimental story about two great painters who were asked to paint a picture entitled "Peace." One painted a beautiful clear lake, with mountains in the background reflected in the lake, which was so perfectly calm that not the slightest ripple disturbed the mirror image. The other painted a waterfall, turbulent and plunging, so that when you looked at it you could almost hear the crash of water on the rocks at the bottom. And on a ledge in the rock-face behind the waterfall was a bird nest and a mother bird feeding her fledglings.

It was suggested that the second more truly portrayed the meaning of peace for Christians. Jesus did not promise freedom from the turmoils of the world but a haven in the midst of the turmoils.

One could perhaps say the same of the Buddha. But the *Dhammapada* portrays the wise man as "clear and peaceful like a lake." And that leads one to conclude that in the Buddhist case the first picture may be more appropriate. In the Buddhist path, the transformation is so profound that all you can see at the end is a perfectly calm lake, or an image of the Buddha sitting in meditation, the perfect picture of peace with a human face.[26]

The Buddha begins with pain; his end is peace.

II

TEACHER, DANCER, FLUTE PLAYER: LORD KRISHNA

TEN READINGS FROM THE *BHAGAVAD GITA*

The Indestructible Soul

He is not born, nor does he ever die,
nor having come to be will he ever cease to be.
Unborn, constant, eternal, that ancient one
is not slain when the body is slain.

As a man casts off worn-out clothes,
and puts on other new ones,
so casting off worn-out bodies,
the embodied soul enters other new ones.

Him no weapon cuts down,
him no fire burns,
water does not wet him
nor do winds dry him.

(2.20,22–23)

Action and Bondage

Therefore, unattached, ever perform
the action that must be performed.
For the man who, unattached, performs action,
obtains the highest.

Better one's own dharma, though imperfect,
than another's dharma well performed.
Better to die within the sphere of one's own dharma;
another's dharma is fraught with danger.

(3.19,35)

The Lord's Acts

Unborn am I, and immutable is my nature
and I am Lord of beings.
Yet resorting to material nature,
I come into being by my own creative power.

For whenever there is
a decline of dharma . . .
and adharma raises its head,
then I send myself forth.

For the protection of the good,
for the destruction of evildoers,
for the sake of the establishment of dharma,
I come into being in age after age.

(4.5–8)

Nonattachment

When all a person's undertakings
are freed from desire or intention,
and his actions are burned up in the fire of wisdom—
the enlightened ones call him a pandit.

Having abandoned all attachment
to the fruits of action,
ever contented, nondependent,
though engaged in actions,
he does nothing at all.

Expecting nothing, his mind and soul restrained,
having abandoned all possessions,
doing only bodily actions,
he does not incur guilt.

Content in taking whatever comes by chance,
having passed beyond the pairs, knowing no envy,
the same in success and failure—
even though acting, he is not bound.

(4.19–22)

The Yogi

The yogi should constantly control himself,
remaining in a private place, alone,
his thoughts and self restrained,
without expectations and possessions.

Having set in a clean place
a firm seat for himself,
neither too high nor too low,
covered with a cloth, a skin, or kusha *grass,*

There let him sit, making the mind one-pointed,
restraining the motions of thought and senses,
and engage in yoga
for the purification of the Self.

Holding body, head, and neck in a straight line
and remaining motionless,
let him fix his gaze on the tip of his nose,
not looking round about him.

With tranquil self, his fear all gone,
firm in his vow of chastity,
holding the mind in control, thinking on me,
there let him sit, integrated, on me intent.

The yogi who, ever thus
with mind restrained integrates himself,
comes to the peace that culminates in nirvana,
which abides in me.

Of all yogis,
he whose inmost self is gone to me,

he who in faith worships me—
he is regarded by me as the most disciplined.

(6.10–15; 47)

The Lord and the World

There is nothing whatever
higher than I, Dhananjaya.
This entire universe is strung on me
like clustered pearls on a thread.

In water, I am taste;
I am the light of the moon and the sun,
the sacred syllable [OM] in all the Vedas,
sound in ether, manliness in man.

The odor in earth am I,
and brilliance in fire;
life in all beings
and asceticism in ascetics am I.

(7.7–9)

Bhakti

Votaries of the gods go to the gods.
Votaries of the ancestors, to the ancestors go.
To the disembodied beings go those who worship them.
But those who sacrifice to me come to me.

When one offers to me with devotion
a leaf or a flower, fruit or water,
that gift of the zealous one I accept—
for it was given in love.

Whatever you do, whatever you eat,
whatever you offer as an oblation,
whatever you give, whatever austerities you practice,
son of Kunti, do it as an offering to me.

For if they take refuge in me, O son of Pritha,
even those who are of lowly origin—
women or Vaishyas or Shudras—
arrive at the supreme goal.

(9.25–27; 32)

The Divine Pervading Powers

Come, I will tell you
of my divine pervading powers—
those at least that are fundamental, O best of Kurus,
for there is no end to the details.

I am the Self [Atman], O Gudakesha,
abiding in the heart of all beings.
I am the beginning and middle and also
the end of beings.

Among the Adityas, I am Vishnu;
of lights the radiant sun.
Of the Maruts, I am Marici.
Of night lights, I am the moon.

Of the Vedas, I am the Samaveda;
of gods, I am Indra, the king of gods.

(10.19–22)

Krishna's Form as the Lord

Many his mouths and eyes,
many his wondrous aspects;
many his divine adornments;
and he brandished many celestial weapons.

He wore celestial garlands and robes,
and was anointed with divine scented ointments.
The All-Wonderful infinite God was he,
facing in every direction.

If the splendor of a thousand suns should burst forth
all at once, in the sky,
it would resemble the splendor
of that exalted one.

There in the body of the God of gods,
the son of Pandu [Arjuna] saw then the whole universe—
a unity, but comprising
a myriad different parts.

(11.10–13)

Krishna's Friendly Form

Therefore I bow myself, prostrate my body,
and crave grace of you, the Lord worthy of praise.
As father with son, as friend with friend,
as lover with beloved,
so I pray you bear with me, O God.

Having seen what has not been seen before,
I am ecstatic, though my heart trembles with fear.
Show me the same form that you had before, O God.
Be gracious, Lord of gods, home of the universe.

(11.44–45)[27]

Another Way: Devotion to Krishna

There is little doubt about the historicity of Gautama. It is generally accepted by scholars that he was born about 560 B.C. at a place called Kapilavastu in southern Nepal. The tradition that he lived into old age and died when he was about eighty is also usually accepted.

About Krishna there is much less certainty. The first appearance of the name is in one of the Upanishads that date from about the time of the Buddha. But there are no details of his life until the great epic of India, the *Mahabharata*, which scholars believe was put together between 300 B.C. and 300 A.D. The central action of the *Mahabharata* is a great war that took place between two sets of cousins, the five Pandavas and the hundred Kauravas. The Pandavas are the good heroes of the epic, and they eventually win the battle. One of the kings who helps the Pandavas to win is Krishna, the king of a people called the Yadavas.

Traditional dating by Indians places the war of the *Mahabharata* well before 1000 B.C., and modern scholars have come to accept that there may well have been something of an epic battle between various tribes that had settled in the western part of the Indo-Gangetic plain in the period between 1800 and 1000 B.C.

But whether any of the details of the life of Krishna in the texts are accurate is impossible to verify. Within the *Mahabharata* there appear to be various strands of tradition interwoven to portray Krishna as a great hero, and beyond that, as God. But what are usually accepted as the major events of Krishna's life by later devotees of Krishna are either omitted altogether, or touched on in brief, passing references. The latter are sufficient to suggest that stories had begun to develop around the hero regarding his remarkable childhood, a common motif for heroes in all cultures (see Campbell, 318–34).

It is generally accepted that the strong interest in the life of Krishna that one can see among devotees of Krishna today—especially in stories of his childhood and youth—developed rather later than the time of the *Mahabharata;* that what is built into these stories is very much dependent upon a theoretical position developed within the *Mahabharata,* in a very short text of eighteen chapters called the *Bhagavad Gita,* "the song of the Blessed One." In this text Krishna is portrayed as a teacher, who presents his teaching to his friend, Arjuna, one of the Pandava brothers. The *Bhagavad Gita,* which scholars customarily date somewhere about the time of Jesus (give or take a hundred years or so), could not possibly date from the time when Krishna was supposed to have lived, for there is much in the text that suggests a response to the Buddhist movement and other related Hindu movements.

In addition, there are features, which can be dated from other sources—Buddhist texts, archeological materials—that point to movements not long before the Christian era.

Thus scholars have generally accepted that in the *Bhagavad Gita* there is presented as the teaching of Krishna a highly significant vision of how one should live—as it was developed among Hindus who attached themselves to Krishna.

The setting of the *Bhagavad Gita* is one that is ever with us—war! The greatest warrior of the epic, the third of the five Pandava brothers, Arjuna, is sitting in his chariot as the great battle is about to begin. He is talking to his friend and charioteer, Krishna, and he says quite bluntly that he does not want to fight. This is, of course, not a surprising state of affairs—we know well that many soldiers are quite fearful before battle begins. But this is not the case with Arjuna. Great hero that he is, he is not afraid to die. His unwillingness to fight is due to the fact that in the opposing army are many of his relatives:

> Krishna, having seen these kinsmen assembled, eager to fight, my limbs grow faint, and my mouth becomes parched, my body trembles and my hair stands on end. My bow falls from my hand, and my skin is on fire. I am unable to stand up. My mind seems to reel. I see adverse omens, Keshava, and I cannot foresee any good at all from slaying my kinsmen in battle. I desire not victory, Krishna—nor kingdom nor pleasures. What is the use of kingdom to us, Govinda? What is the use of delights or life? For the sake of whom kingdom, delights and pleasures are desired by us—these stand ready to surrender life and wealth in battle: teachers, fathers, sons and grandfathers too—and uncles, fathers-in-law, grandsons, brothers-in-law, and other relatives. Though they slay me I would not want to kill them, even for dominion over the three worlds—how much less for the sake of this earth! [*Bhagavad Gita,* 1.28–35].

Arjuna feels that there is something peculiarly inhuman about killing one's kin. He even suggests that it would be better to become a *bhikshu,* a monk like the Buddha, than to kill his teachers.

Just as the Buddhist teaching is predicated upon an extreme version of the facts of existence, here too it is an extreme situation that forms the backdrop and the stimulus for a general view, in the form of a new message, of the way one ought to live. Krishna's first words in response to Arjuna's troubled statement are aimed at allaying Arjuna's fears about killing. But as he does so, he plunges us into a view of how to live that has a much wider application than the situation of a battle. For Krishna takes seriously Arjuna's desire to become a *bhikshu* and sets out to show why the life of a *bhikshu* is unnecessary for Arjuna, and also for others. Using the idea of rebirth, the idea that living beings are born over and over again into different bodily forms—an idea that we have seen in somewhat different form from Buddhists—he argues first that the embodied one, the real person, does not die. The true self is not burned when the body is burned, is not killed when the body is killed. The real person, the true self, has no beginning. Depending on an idea of "conservation of souls"—a kind of parallel to the belief in the conservation of matter—Krishna argues that, like matter, beings that acquire an embodied form cannot be created or destroyed. They are eternal, imperishable, immutable.

So Arjuna, says Krishna, should not worry about what he must do. He is a warrior and his duty is to fight. If he must kill in time of war, he can take consolation in the fact that the real self does not die. Arjuna, then, need not become a monk.

But Krishna, having indicated what Arjuna should do in this specific extreme situation, then launches into a discussion of what one should do, how one should live in more general terms. His discussion is set against the background of accepted ideas about the nature of bondage, the bondage of being reborn over and over again. This was one of the major ways, as we have seen, in which both Buddhists and orthodox Hindu writers had framed the problem of the painfulness of existence.

The analysis of the *Bhagavad Gita* depends upon the distinction between the body and the embodied one, between souls and the material universe to which they are bound. The source of bondage is found, according to Krishna, in one of the three *gunas* or "strands" of *prakriti,* the stuff from which the material universe is derived. The multifarious and discrete phenomena of the universe are each seen as due to the predominance of one or other of these three strands—goodness, passion or energy, and darkness or inertia. Krishna argues that it is desire and its negative face, anger, both sprung from the strand of passion or energy, that cause attachment, and this is what keeps the embodied one embodied, bound to matter. But then he gives another explanation: actions happen at the level of these strands of matter, but those who are deluded by a sense of individuality think that *they* perform actions, and thus they become entangled with the actions in which their bodily form is engaged.

The classical picture of how bondage takes place is given in the Upanishads and is related to the law of karma (work, action), according to which one is reborn to a good or a bad condition in a future life in accordance with one's actions in this life. The earliest statement of this picture is given in the *Chandogya Upanishad,* 5.10.7:

Those whose conduct on earth has given pleasure, can hope to enter a pleasant womb, that is, the womb of a Brahman, or a woman of the princely class; but those whose conduct on earth has been foul can expect to enter a foul and stinking womb, that is, the womb of a bitch or a pig or an outcaste [Zaehner, 101].

An alternative upanishadic discussion, however, is the one that the *Bhagavad Gita* follows:

As a man acts, as he behaves, so does he become. Whoso does good, becomes good: who so does evil, becomes evil. By good works a man becomes good, by evil works he becomes evil. But some have said: "This 'person' consists of desire alone. As is his desire, so will his will be; as is his will, so will he act; as he acts, so will he attain" [*Brihadaranyaka Upanishad,* 4.4.5 (Zaehner, 71)].

This takes action back to its motivation. Action ultimately depends on desire. It is where one's desires are, where one is attached, that one goes:

To what his mind and character are attached,
To that attached a man goes with his works.
Whatever deeds he does on earth,
Their rewards he reaps.
From the other world he comes back here—
To the world of deed and work.

So much for the man of desire.

Now we come to the man without desire:

He is devoid of desire, free from desire; all his desires have been fulfilled: the Self alone is his desire. His bodily functions do not depart when he departs this world. Being very Brahman to Brahman does he go.

On this there is this verse:

> When all desires which shelter in the heart
> Detach themselves then does a mortal man
> Become immortal: to Brahman he wins through
> [*Brihadaranyaka Upanishad,* 4.4.6–7 (Zaehner, 71)].

The *Bhagavad Gita* argument is similar to this. If one is to be free, what is needed is detachment. By desire and anger persons are attached to things, other persons, actions, and it is this that binds them. If one is to be free, one should act without attachment, live without attachment. Focusing things at the level of desire and attachment, Krishna is able to say that one should do one's caste duty—but without attachment. Better one's own duty performed imperfectly than someone else's well done.

It is interesting that the analysis in terms of passion and desire as the cause of attachment is not far from that of Buddhists. But the way to free oneself from bondage is quite different from that of Buddhists, or the Upanishads, or the law books of the Brahmans, or the other heterodox sects of India such as the Jains. All of these groups were convinced that in order to be free from the effects of *karma,* one had to a greater or lesser extent give up *karma,* works. One had to live a life away from the ordinary with its rush and bustle. The search for liberation involved a life of inactivity in the forest or the wilderness. One had to become a monk or a *sannyasin.*[28] In the suggestion of the *Gita* that one can find liberation even while living an ordinary life of action, a new message is being offered.[29]

The term developed to talk of this way of unattached action was *karma-yoga* (the discipline of action), which is contrasted with *karma-sannyasa* (the laying aside, or renunciation, of action). In presenting this new path the *Gita* does not deny the validity of the older path. Both lead to freedom. The *Gita* does suggest

the superiority of karma-yoga on the grounds that one whose renunciation is firm neither hates nor desires; that is, the crucial
point about a *sannyasin* is that he is a karma-yogi. The argument
here in favor of karma-yoga is that detachment is the most basic
element, all that is necessary.

But the *Gita* is nothing if not unclear about the precise relationship between the various religious practices that had by this time
been developed in India. Different terms are used for the same
path: the major way developed in the Upanishads—in which one
gives up ordinary life and goes out to live in the forest to meditate
and search for wisdom—is referred to in the *Gita* as renunciation
of action, *samkhya,* and knowledge or wisdom. And these are
variously related to yoga—the first and third are said to be inferior to yoga, the second is said to be not different from yoga. In
addition it appears that the term "yoga" is used in different
ways—as a short form for karma-yoga, the path of disciplined
action; but also to refer to what is more traditionally meant by
this term—a system of physical and psychic discipline leading into
meditation. In general, it seems that the *Gita* wants to assert the
validity of all paths but also uphold a new path of yoga. From the
way the *Gita* moves its argument forward, little by little, it appears that the path envisioned is one in which the yogi lives a
disciplined life of unattached action focused on the practice of
yogic meditation.[30]

But then another new path is added. It is introduced by the
intimation that the truly yogic yogi is the one who in faith worships Krishna! But then, in another step, this way of devotion is
taken out of the context of yoga altogether. One may obtain liberation by simple devotion to Krishna. Even an evil person; even
people on their deathbeds; even those "of base origin," such
as men of the lower castes and women—all these may obtain
freedom by seeking refuge in Krishna. Simple offerings of a leaf,
a flower, fruit, or water given in love are accepted by Krishna.

Actions of this latter kind can be seen today in houses and temples and small wayside shrines of snake deities and tree deities all
over India. One finds oneself wondering if all this devotional activity began with this text; or was the text simply a response to a
style of religiousness already practiced by many Indians, particularly those of the lower classes?

There are enough suggestions in the *Gita* itself to support the latter proposition: that the prior practice of making offerings to deities was in the *Gita* given new depth, in that it proclaimed that those who offer their devotion to Krishna may thereby find salvation from the ocean of *samsara*, the continuous onward flow of births and deaths.

That Krishna can offer liberation to those who turn to him is predicated upon another very important strand of thought in the *Gita*. It is regularly accepted within Indian mythology that deities have certain powers, areas of effective control within the universe. It is important to note that from the earliest strands of Indian literature one finds a system that might be described as polytheistic—with many deities, each associated with particular physical phenomena, each with limited powers associated with these phenomena.[31] Thus a woman longing for a son, might appropriately approach a deity with powers in relation to fertility—perhaps a snake deity, or a deity indwelling a large tree.

That Krishna can offer liberation from the world of *samsara* is dependent on who he is. For it is clear that the *Bhagavad Gita* does not present Krishna as just a charioteer or even a great military hero or a king.

Krishna is the being whom we would call God. He is all and all is in him. He supports the entire universe with a small portion of himself. He is the origin of all—including the gods and the three strands of the material universe (which he brings into being by means of his creative power). He is the essence of all things; in terms of speculation that had been accepted by this time, he is the essence of water, which is taste; the essence of man, which is manliness; the essence of luminous bodies, which is light; and so on.[32] In addition there is a section in which he is portrayed as the best of every conceivable class of beings—they are his glorious manifestations; one might say that if one wants to penetrate to his nature, one may begin by looking at the chief or best example of a class of beings. Above all, he is the Supreme Person; there is none higher than he.

But how can this charioteer and friend of Arjuna be God? Quite early in the argument of the *Gita*, in the discussion about unattached action, there is an indication that action is appropriate rather than inaction, because, Krishna indicates, *he* is continually involved in action. And then there is introduced the germ of the doctrine on the basis of which one may understand that Krishna is God. Krishna says that in age after age, when there is a rising up of *adharma* (lack of virtue) and a decline of virtue (*dharma*), he comes into the world, he assumes a mundane form. The picture seems to be that he who is the creator and sustainer of the universe finds it necessary on occasion, when the stability of the worlds is threatened by negative powers, to assume a terrestrial form in order to redress the balance. What we have here is the beginning of the doctrine of *avatara*, "incarnation," or, more literally, "descent." (The word *avatara* is not used, however.) No details of such descents are given in the *Gita*, but in later literature there are developed many lists of avatars. Eventually a more or less standard picture emerges of ten major avatars, though there is never complete agreement on what the ten are. But in the *Gita* itself the idea functions to explain how this human Krishna can also call himself God, or, better, how the Supreme Person comes to be in this human form of the friend and charioteer of Arjuna.

After a great deal of teaching, much of it startlingly new, the central argument of the *Bhagavad Gita* is brought to a fine climax when Krishna unveils himself to Arjuna in his form as Ishvara, the Supreme Lord. It is a magnificent vision, and Arjuna is dazzled by the splendor as he sees a being with myriads of mouths, arms, eyes, and weapons, who contains within himself the entire universe. Arjuna is able to see the process of the creation and dissolution of the universe. Eventually the whole picture is so majestic as to be profoundly terrifying, and Arjuna asks Krishna to assume again his old friendly form. And Krishna obliges.

There has been an enormous amount of debate over the years about what is the central message of the *Bhagavad Gita*. It seems to me that the *Gita* sets forth a number of paths to freedom, and argues for the legitimacy of all of them—the way of renunciation coupled with the knowledge that one's innermost Self is identical with the ultimate Self of the universe; the way of disciplined action; the discipline of yoga, as an extension or as a central focus of the way of disciplined action; and the way of devotion to God. If one accepts the sheer weight of emphasis, the *Bhagavad Gita* appears to be centered on a path of disciplined action, which includes the practice of yoga meditation, and is brought to its fulfillment in worship of Krishna.

"To Be the Breath in His Flute"

The subsequent portrayal of the life of Krishna is related to the way of devotion, to the theme of the relationship between God and his devotees. The events of his life were first set forth in a continuous narrative shortly after the completion of the compilation of the *Mahabharata*, and they were added as an appendix to it. The work thus constructed, called the *Harivamsha*, was soon followed by another that appears to be an attempt to refine somewhat the rather rough folkloric texture of the *Harivamsha* stories. This text, the *Vishnu Purana*, is not nearly so colorful as the *Harivamsha*, and seems to be more concerned with the *implications* of the life of Krishna. A few hundred years later another major text, the *Bhagavata Purana*, recounts in detail the life of Krishna.[33] This is clearly the most beautiful version and it became a favorite all over India. It adds new stories and new motifs to the account of Krishna, and as well incorporates into the account a well-developed theology.

The life of Krishna as it is presented in these texts is, in briefest form, as follows. The wicked king Kamsa heard a prophecy that the eighth child of his cousin, Devaki, would be responsible for his death. He determined to kill her, but Devaki's husband managed to persuade Kamsa to spare her on condition that he deliver to Kamsa every child born to Devaki.

Meanwhile, many wicked kings are oppressing the earth (one of them is Kamsa); these kings are really demons who have undertaken birth as humans. The goddess Earth eventually seeks help from the gods, who form a deputation and go off to visit the supreme deity, Vishnu. Vishnu promises that he will be born on earth as two brothers, Balarama and Krishna. The embryo that is Balarama is removed from the womb of Devaki before birth, so that he is born of a cowherd woman, Rohini. When Krishna is born, he is taken at night by his father, Vasudeva, from the prison where Kamsa has kept him along with Devaki. The doors of the prison miraculously open while the guards sleep. Vasudeva leaves the city of Mathura and goes across the Yamuna River to a cowherd village named Gokula, where a young woman named Yashoda, the wife of the chief of the village, has just given birth to a baby girl. Vasudeva, while everyone sleeps, goes into the house and exchanges the babies. Returning to Mathura he takes the baby girl into the prison. When Kamsa hears about the birth of a baby, he comes to the prison, takes the child, and smashes its head against a rock. Immediately the baby disappears and a goddess appears and predicts that Devaki's eighth child, now born but safe from Kamsa, will one day kill him.

The story that follows is of the childhood and youth of Krishna living in disguise among the cowherd people. He kills many demons who trouble the people. A number of demons are sent by Kamsa to get rid of him. These demons take different forms—a crane, a whirlwind, a bull, a large serpentine figure. A great deal of attention is also given to Krishna's boyish pranks, to his play with other young cowherd boys, in the *Bhagavata Purana* to his flute, and to his amorous adventures with the women of the village as he blossoms into early adolescence. But eventually he returns to Mathura, kills Kamsa, and becomes king in his stead. There follow many details of his life as king but these have never greatly captured the imagination of his devotees. The significant events for them are those of his childhood and youth.

We thus have a very different state of affairs from the life of Gautama. The quest motif of the hero stories is absent from the life of Krishna. The battle motif is there, in multiple form, for he is continually overcoming threatening demonic figures. But this is not a fighting of battles in order to reach a goal; rather it is the one who is himself the goal, battling against the negative forces of the universe. We can see in the traditions about the Buddha the development of birth/childhood narratives that utilize the common hero motif of the amazing powers of the heroic child, in such a way that they are merely an assertion of the great significance of the life of the Buddha. But with Krishna his marvelous childhood becomes the center of attention. And the stories do not function just to underline the significance of Krishna's life or message. Rather, it is accepted from the outset that he is God, the supreme Lord Vishnu, who has undertaken a descent onto the mundane plane. So the stories are liberated to portray something very different: as I have already suggested, they explore the nature of God and his relationship with his devotees.

Initially, as in the case of other stories of avatars of Vishnu, the many accounts of overcoming demons serve as a narrative commentary on Krishna's statement in the *Bhagavad Gita* that for the establishment of virtue, for the protection of the good and for the destruction of the evil, he comes into being in age after age. In many puranic texts, the idea of a decline in dharma [virtue] and of the rising up of its opposite, *adharma*, is correlated with the taking over of the world by demons. In the account of Krishna, this idea is focused on the wicked king, Kamsa, but there is an extension beyond this to suggest that with Kamsa in power, demonic forces are wreaking havoc on the world. Thus initially the overcoming of many demons is a restoring of order to the world, a protection of the world from calamity.

The implication of this kind of activity is the portrayal of Krishna as one who can save, one who will protect, one to whom one can safely go for refuge. This aspect is further underlined in a story of Krishna's swallowing up of a forest fire, thus saving cows and cowherds from a terrible death. One can see the same in his holding up Mount Govardhana to protect persons and cows from rains that pour down for seven days and threaten to inundate the village. (These rains are sent in anger by the king of the gods, Indra, because Krishna has suggested to the villagers that they make their offerings to him and not Indra; Indra in a fit of pique resolves to punish the villagers. Krishna takes the mountain and holds it up so that it becomes a massive umbrella for all the villagers and their cows.

In the *Bhagavata Purana*, however, another dimension is added to some of the stories of demonic and other dangerous figures. One very well known account is that of the great female demon Putana.

The story as told in *Bhagavata* is basically the same as earlier accounts in the *Harivamsha* and the *Vishnu Purana*. Putana comes at night to kill the infant Krishna; having placed poison on her breasts she goes to suckle him. She appears in the form of a beautiful young woman and everybody thinks she is Vishnu's consort, Shri, come to visit her husband, so she easily gains access to the baby. When Krishna sucks, however, he is unharmed by the poison; moreover, he sucks the life out of her.

A new section is added to the story in *Bhagavata*: Putana's body is cut up and cremated:

From the body of Putana when it was burned
smoke arose fragrant as sandalwood:
her sins had been destroyed
since she had suckled Krishna.
The blood-sucking *rakshasi,* Putana,
devourer of children and men
gave her breast to Krishna, intent upon killing him—
and obtained bliss! [10.6.34–35].

Putana, although with evil intent, performs actions that are those
of a mother—and so is saved.
The *Bhagavata* gives an alternative explanation of why Putana
is saved:

His feet abide in the hearts of his devotees,
his feet are honoured by those honoured among men;
with those feet he trod on her body
when he sucked her breast [10.6.37].

Putana in her act of suckling Krishna is blessed by the touch of
Krishna's feet. Before discussing the implications of these statements, it is worthwhile to consider another story, that of
Krishna's taming of the great serpent king, Kaliya, who lives in
the Yamuna River, and so pollutes the water with poison that
cows and cowherds die. Krishna decides to get rid of him, so he
jumps into the water, right into Kaliya's lair, and a terrible battle
begins. At first it appears that the little Krishna, just six years old,
is going to be easily crushed in the coils of the great snake. The
villagers who come rushing down to the river are sick with anx-
iety. But Krishna is teasing them. His apparently dangerous situation is one that increases the intensity of their devotion to him.
Eventually Krishna frees himself from the serpent's coils. He then
proceeds to tame Kaliya:

Like the king of birds
Krishna moved playfully around the serpent.
The serpent also moved
awaiting an opportunity to strike.

When the serpent tired
the Primal One bent the serpent's neck
and mounted his hood.
Then the supreme teacher of all arts
began to dance,
his lotus feet coppery
with the luster of the numerous jewels
on the serpent's head.
Seeing him ready to dance
the wives of Gandharvas, Siddhas, Suras, Caranas, and
    Devas,
suddenly approached him,
playing in delight
on different kinds of drums
and other instruments,
praising him with songs
and with gifts of flowers.
The chastizer of the wicked
trampled under foot
the heads of the hundred-headed serpent.
Vomiting blood from mouth and nose
the serpent lost consciousness—
sinking under the heavy weight of Krishna
bearing within himself
the entire universe [*Bhagavata*, 10.16.25–28].

Kaliya, however, is not destroyed. Instead he is sent off to a
place where he can live without endangering the lives of other
creatures. The water of the Yamuna becomes free from poison.
    That Kaliya is not killed is due in part, it would appear, to a
prayer for forgiveness, offered by the wives of Kaliya to Krishna.
In the process of this prayer, the wives draw the most unexpected
implications concerning the dancing of Krishna on Kaliya's head:

Those who find refuge in the dust of your feet
long not for heaven
nor to be world emperor nor to rule in Rasatala.
Not yogic powers do they desire
nor even freedom from rebirth.

This lord of serpents, sprung from *tamas,*
the embodiment of wrath,
has obtained that which is so difficult to obtain.
There is supreme bliss for him now,
such as he desires—even while he lives
revolving on the wheel of rebirth
                    [*Bhagavata*, 10.16.36–38].

From these and from other similar accounts of enemies of
Krishna who are killed by him and thus saved, it becomes ap-
parent that in the *Bhagavata Purana* the manifestation of Krishna
as upholder of goodness and protector of those who turn to him is
not the primary function of the stories about demons. The classic
interpretation of the change comes from a verse in which the sage
Narada explains why it is that someone like Kamsa, an enemy of
the Lord, should be saved:

Concentrating their minds on the Lord
through desire, hatred, fear, affection or devotion,
and having laid aside evil,
many have gone to his abode [*Bhagavata*, 7.1.29].

According to Narada, anything that binds one to the Lord in
one's thoughts, anything that normally characterizes an intense
or close relationship between two persons, so that they are always
in each other's thoughts—whether such a characteristic has a positive or negative tone—is able to bring a person to liberation.
There is even the strong suggestion by Narada that a negative
relationship is more effective for the gaining of liberation than is a
positive one:

It is my firm opinion
that a mortal does not so easily attain to unity with God
through devotion as through the arising of enmity
                    [*Bhagavata*, 7.1.26].

The *Bhagavata* does not always, however, elevate negative relationships above positive ones. At times the negative is used as a
contrast to a more acceptable positive relationship, as in the final
comment on the Putana story:

How much more shall he obtain bliss
who gives with faith and devotion
his dearest and best to Krishna, the soul supreme.
And what of those attached to him
like a mother? [10.6.36].

The *Bhagavata* has transformed these stories in such a way that
the essential requirement for liberation is to be attached to
Krishna, to focus one's life on him—and knowing that hatred can
be more intense than love, it suggests that the enemies of the Lord
may as well attain to him as his devotees. In a sense, the only sin
for the *Bhagavata* poet is to be indifferent toward Krishna.

Much of the story can be seen as a demonstration of the ways in
which in his grace Krishna shows himself to the cowherds and
their cows in order to draw forth from them a response—be it
wonder, love, joy, fear, awe. A feature that accentuates the element of wonder is a juxtaposition that is frequently made between
the smallness of the child and his greatness as God. Just as Christian theologians have often wondered at the paradox of "the
Word unable to speak a word," God become a baby in a manger
at Bethlehem, so also the devotees of Krishna have built into their
stories the paradox already inherent in the *Bhagavad Gita*
portrayal of Krishna in his awesome form as the Lord of the universe, and his friendly form as the charioteer of Arjuna. One of
the most telling portrayals of this is the time when Krishna's foster mother, Yashoda, looks into his mouth after his brother Balarama reports to her that the little Krishna has been stuffing
himself with earth:

When she said, "Very well, open it!"
He, the blessed Hari, the Supreme Lord,
who had in sport taken the form of a young child,
opened his mouth.
She saw there the whole universe—
the sky and the quarters,
the great divisions of the world
with the mountains and oceans
and the circle of the earth,
and wind and fire,
and the moon and the stars;

the sun, the zodiac, water, light, air and sky;
the restless senses, the mind, matter, and the three strands.
Seeing in the body of her son
this wonderful universe . . .
and seeing there even Vraja,
and herself,
she shook with terror.

"Is this a dream?
Is it the wondrous power of God?
Or is it alas the infatuation of my own mind?
Or is it my child who is the origin of it?
With his own yoga?
I bow down to the feet of that one
who is not within the realm of comprehension,
who cannot be grasped by the intellect,
by the mind, by actions, or by speech;
who is the refuge of all;
by whom and from whom
the utterly inconceivable universe originates"
                    [*Bhagavata Purana*, 10.8.36–41].

Clearly a marvelous vision! Magnificent in its intensity. But perhaps what is most outstanding is the way it takes a natural response of parents to their children and directs it toward Krishna. For what parent has not been overawed in the presence of the miracle of the baby—the dance of a finger in the air, the peace of a toe finding a mouth, the first glimmer of a smile—what parent has not been struck silent with wonder at this marvel more profound than all the worlds?

The modes of this wonder work in different ways. Sometimes, as here, it is the wonder that this child is the Lord of all the worlds; at other times, no less a wonder that this immensely powerful one has deigned to submit himself to the form of a tiny baby:

In his birth as the Boar
the immeasurable oceans were incapable
of filling even a hair follicle.

Yet Yashoda bathed
the Lord of lotus eyes
with water held in her two hands
[*Krishnakarnamrita*, 2.27].

The paradox is also utilized effectively in the story of Kaliya; in the section cited, Kaliya succumbs to Krishna, the child who bears within him all the worlds.

Another feature of the Kaliya story is the portrayal of Krishna as dancer. And one of the amazing features of the story of Krishna, particularly as it is presented in the *Bhagavata Purana*, is the concentration on a variety of his playful activities. There is much attention to his playing in the dirt, his hanging on the tails of calves, his stealing of butter, his dancing a twinkle-toes dance—all when he is just a toddler, and always around him are the *gopis*, the cowherd women, who are enchanted—sometimes annoyed, but always enchanted—by his mischievous play. As he grows older he goes off with the cowherd boys whose task it is to care for the calves during the day, and there are many pictures of their romping in the woods. Krishna takes up the flute at this stage, and this leads into a new phase: the distant sound of his flute as he returns in the evening becomes a sign to the *gopis* that he is home, and they rush out to greet him.

Gradually there is a portrayal of the developing erotic love of the *gopis* for Krishna, and the flute becomes the initial stimulus arousing their desire. But not only the *gopis* are affected. As with the other play of Krishna, the flute arouses in all creatures wonder, love, infatuation. Peacocks dance, goddesses lose all self-respect, cows stand caressing Krishna in their minds, their eyes moist with tears. All creatures are delighted by the sound of the flute:

It arouses the world, makes the Veda echo its sound:
it gladdens the trees, and causes the mountains to totter,
enchants the deer, and transports with rapture the cows.
Bewildering the cowherds, sending sages into *samadhi*,
by its seven notes it utters the true meaning of OM:
Thus trills the Flute of the Child
[*Krishnakarnamrita*, 2.110].

And not only his childish pranks and his flute playing and his boyish games, but also his heroic deeds of slaying demons and lifting Mount Govardhana become subsumed within the portrayal of his life as *lila*, "play". For these are child's play to him. But like the other playful acts they become the means whereby he draws all to him.

The relationship of Krishna to the *gopis* merits attention as a particular focus of his play. The beginning of the more erotic stage of this is seen in the episode where he steals the clothes of the young *gopis* who have left them on the bank of the river while they bathe. He collects the clothes, climbs into a tree with them, and then makes each girl come begging him for her sari. There are many pictures of the growing attachment of the women to Krishna: they are overjoyed when he is with them, they pine for him all day when he is off with the cowherd boys, and in his absence they sing songs about him, about his enchanting beauty and his marvelous deeds.

The climax of the story of Krishna among the cowherd people is the account of the dance that he dances with the *gopis* by the light of the autumn moon. Wanting to dance, he plays his flute and the women are drawn irresistibly to him. The theme of separation is introduced again as he goes off with one special *gopi* and the others are left pining for him. They go in search of him. But unable to find him, in his absence they again recall his play, acting out major events of his life. Finally, he returns and explains that he withholds himself from those he loves in order to increase their love. Then he dances with them in a circle, multiplying himself in such a way that each of the women imagines that she alone is dancing with Krishna. At the end he dallies along the banks of the river, and bathes with them in the waters of the Yamuna River.

A question, easily raised, about the morality of all this is answered in the *Bhagavata Purana* most cogently in the suggestion that Krishna's erotic play with the *gopis*, like his other play, has no selfish motive, for he, God, is self-fulfilled. His descent is motivated by his desire to manifest his grace, to call forth wonder, awe, joy, and love in those who see his play.

As one sees Krishna playing in the dirt, stealing butter, dancing his dances, and hears him playing his haunting flute, one cannot but respond in wonder and love and joy. And gradually the light dawns—God in his profound love takes the form of a child, a concrete focus for devotion. And the *gopi*s are, in the intensity of their attachment to Krishna, models for devotees.[34]

The ramifications of the story of Krishna continued to grow in the period following that of the Puranas. In a flourishing tradition in Bengal, a great deal of attention was given to differentiating stages of devotion. There were five of them, the last three following the words of Arjuna in the *Bhagavad Gita*, "As father with son, as friend with friend, as lover with beloved, so I pray you bear with me, O God." It was argued that the highest form of *bhakti* (devotion) was on the analogy of lover and beloved. And then a new set of stories was developed and explored, having to do with the relationship between Krishna and one particular *gopi* who was his favorite—Radha. The course of their love is sketched in poem after poem. But the course of true love never runs smooth, and the theme of separation is deepened by a portrayal of Krishna as a fickle youth who runs off after other women. But in the end he returns and they are together:

The moon has shone upon me,
the face of my beloved.
O night of joy!

Joy permeates all things.
My life: joy
my youth: fulfillment.
Today my house is again
home,
    today my body is
my body.

    The god
of destiny smiled on me.
No more doubt.

Let the nightingales sing, then,
let there be myriad
rising moons. Let Kama's
five arrows become five thousand

and the south wind
softly, softly blow:
for now my body has meaning
in the presence of my beloved [Dimock and Levertov, 66].

Again Radha says:

As the mirror to my hand,
the flowers to my hair,
kohl to my eyes,
tambul to my mouth,
musk to my breast,
necklace to my throat,
ecstasy to my flesh,
heart to my home—

as wing to bird,
water to fish,
life to the living—
so you to me.
But tell me,
Madhava, beloved,
who are you?
Who are you really? [ibid., 15].

The question at the end suggests that Radha did not know, but may have begun to suspect, what the devotee does know—that, of course, Krishna is God. And then the poem seems to be saying, "As Radha found fulfillment in her lover Krishna, so all find fulfillment in God."

Any Christian will recognize that this is not foreign to the Christian tradition; after all, Saint Augustine said: "Thou hast made us for Thyself, and our hearts are restless until they rest in Thee." But although Christians and others have seen this, never has there been such an imaginative portrayal as this perception of what life is about.

The question about the importance of the historicity of the great religious founder figures was raised earlier. Of none of them are we more doubtful than we are with regard to Krishna. Yet as we ponder these stories we realize how unimportant it is to know whether Krishna did the things we read about or even whether Krishna ever lived. What is significant is the way in which poets have developed the stories of a playful and mischievous child who performs wonders. These stories unveil for humanity the mystery of a God who, in his grace enables one to find fulfillment, to find life in him—in loving him, in performing concrete *acts* of love (offering a leaf or a flower, fruit or water); or just in being his breath:

> I am forever blessed!
> For I am his own breath, within his flute!
> And if that breath is used up, in one song,
> I shall not mourn.
> The joy of all the worlds is in his flute,
> and I his breath!
> Let my song be good or evil,
> let it be played with joy or sorrow,
> I will sound it in the morning,
> and in the evening it will sound,
> and I will play it, softly muffled, in the night.
> I will play it in the spring,
> I will play it in the fall,
> and when his breath is used up, in his song,
> I shall not mourn.
> My song will be the loveliest of songs.
> What more could I want? [Dimock, 270].

III

THE STRAIGHT MAT AND THE UNCARVED BLOCK: MASTER KUNG AND MASTER LAO

TEN SAYINGS FROM THE *ANALECTS*

2.7   *Nowadays a filial son is just a man who keeps his parents in food. But even dogs or horses are given food. If there is no feeling of reverence, wherein lies the difference?*

7.1   *Confucius said: "I am a transmitter and not a creator. I believe in and have a passion for the ancients. I venture to compare myself with our old P'eng [China's Methuselah]."*

7.15   *The Duke of She asked Tzu Lu about Confucius, and Tzu Lu gave him no answer. Confucius said: "Why didn't you tell him that I am a person who forgets to eat when he is enthusiastic about something, forgets all his worries in the enjoyment of it, and is not aware that old age is coming on?"*

8.2   *Courtesy not bounded by the prescriptions of ritual becomes tiresome, caution becomes timidity, daring becomes turbulence, inflexibility becomes harshness.*

10.9   *He must not sit on a mat that is not straight.*

11.11   *Tzu Lu asked about the worship of ghosts and spirits. Confucius said: "We don't yet know how to serve men, how can we know about the serving of spirits?" "What about death," was the next question. Confucius said: "We don't know yet about life, how can we know about death?"*

12.2   *Do not do to others what you would not like yourself.*

12.21   *Fan Chih asked about the meaning of Jen. The Master said, "Love men."*

17.11   *The master said, "Ritual! Ritual! Is it no more than the offering of jade and silk? Music! Music! Is it no more than bells and drums?"*

18.6   *One cannot herd with birds and beasts. If I am not to be a man among other men, then what am I to be? If the Way prevailed under heaven, I should not be trying to alter things.*[35]

"The Three Religions of China"

In attempting to draw forth from the multiplicity of important religious figures of human history a handful that might be called our leading lights, I encountered a number of problems. My initial decision was to focus on founder figures—the founders of the great religions of the world. In many respects that proved fruitful. But as I pursued some thinking about the relationship between the teaching and the life stories of these founders I began to realize that, more so than in the case of second-level figures such as Paul or Augustine or Nagarjuna or al-Ghazzali, the life stories and teachings together presented a distinctive vision, a discovery to which the secondary figures responded. What was most significant was the breakthrough quality of their lives and teaching.

This was a valuable insight in reflection on the Jewish religion, for the founder, strictly speaking, must be Abraham, the father of the people. Yet the *teacher* is Moses. I was able in this instance to push things a little further to argue to myself that in a sense Moses is also the founder: there is enough evidence in the Bible that later teachers—the prophets and others—saw the foundation of their nation in the bringing of the people of Israel out of the land of Egypt by Moses. It could then be argued that Moses was the founder, Abraham a precursor. But it is the *vision* of Moses that is really significant: later Jews have attempted to live their lives in terms of what Moses is seen to have discovered.

In the case of Hindus the problem with founders is of a totally different order. Of the incredibly multifarious religious phenomena that some call "Hinduism"—and that Ninian Smart has recently suggested should be called "a federation of Hinduisms" (Smart, *Search*, 27)—there is no beginning, so there is no founder figure. The choice of Krishna as a representative figure for Hindus was somewhat arbitrary, but was related to the perception that Krishna better than any other figure is able to lead us into central aspects of the religious life of Hindus. A few hundred years after the time of Gautama there was achieved in India a rather grand synthesis that allowed within it considerable diversity. The teaching of the Krishna of the *Bhagavad Gita* is representative of the foundations of this "classical Hinduism." In his distinctive presentation of this synthesis, Krishna, although no founder, is foundational—is clearly a breakthrough figure.

The other breakthrough figure from India, Gautama the Buddha, holds a more or less traditional place as a founder figure, in that there is a movement that is traced back to him and that spread across much of Asia. And this brings us to China. The situation of China is not unlike that of India in that we have here a great culture existing for something like four thousand years, the last two thousand being dominated by three religions—Buddhism, Confucianism, and Taoism—the first originating in India, the other two traceable, according to tradition, to the figures who are the subject of this chapter.

Just as it must be emphasized that to talk of "Hinduism" does little justice to the complexity of Indian religious life over the centuries, so also it must be said that to talk of "the three religions of China" can give a distorting impression (Smith, 60–61, 64–67). For it can be shown that frequently a person in China could participate quite significantly in all three of the major movements. The movements have frequently intertwined, but at other times have provided for different dimensions of religious awareness. So it is valuable to try to be aware of ways in which different and even apparently contradictory views of how human life should be lived can coexist and complement each other. And this we shall attempt.

Master Kung

Master Kung—in Chinese, Kung-tzu or Kung-fu-tzu (latinized to Confucius)—was born, according to Chinese tradition, in 552 or 551 B.C. Modern scholars generally accept that this is accurate. As with the Buddha, the earliest biography dates from some three hundred years after his death. There are earlier texts that give brief details, but even the *Analects*, a collection of sayings by Master Kung (with some of which we began this chapter) is regarded as of uneven value if one is trying to find out just what he was like or what he thought.

The generally accepted biography is briefly as follows. Born in the state of Lu, he lived his early life in comparative poverty. He managed to get involved in the political life of the state, and achieved some small measure of success in politics. His highest position was that of prime minister of Lu. But this was for a short time only, and then he was exiled for thirteen years, during which time he wandered around from court to court looking for a position. He never succeeded in getting one. In his own eyes he was a failure.

During this time of failure, however, he established a private school, one of the first in China. He attracted students solely by force of his own personality and the quality of his teaching. But even here his greatness was not recognized; it was four hundred years before his teaching was widely accepted. According to tradition, he died in 479 B.C., at the age of seventy-two.

The first major thing to notice about his life is that Kung's is one of the great failure-success stories of all history. A failure at politics, where he set his heart, he was a master at the art of teaching. But even here his success was not visible. We shall see that others of our leading lights, according to the traditions, underwent at least a period of failure. The nearest to Kung is Jesus, who suffered a felon's death, surely the fate of a failure. But the shift from failure to success for Kung is nowhere near as dramatic as in the case of Jesus or Muhammad (these are themselves very different, as we shall see). That it is such a gradual shift is fully in keeping with the style and content of his teaching. Nothing startling here, nothing bombastic. The emphasis is upon solidity, upon sure foundations.

The second thing noticeable about his life story is that it lacks just about everything that one finds with Gautama and Krishna. No cosmic dimensions, no childhood marvels, no grand predictions, no quest, no battle against evil powers. All that we are left with is the teacher—in this alone does he resemble the others.

There is a story about Kung which sheds some light on this lack of interest in marvels. It concerns the legendary sage ruler Huang Ti, the "Yellow Lord":

> "Was the Yellow Lord a man or was he not a man?" asks a disciple of Confucius. "How is it that he reached [the age of] three hundred years?" To which Confucius is made to reply that this is a misunderstanding: what is actually meant is that during the Yellow Lord's own life of one hundred years, the people enjoyed his benefits; during the first hundred years after his death, they revered his spirit; and during the next hundred years after that, they continued to follow his teachings. "And this is why there is mention of three hundred years" [Bodde, 373–374].

Derk Bodde, who gives other similar examples, makes the point that Confucian scholars, on account of their strong humanism, tended to be "indifferent towards supernatural matters, or to seek to explain them in purely rationalistic terms" (Bodde, 375). And this is in keeping with the teaching of Kung. Of all the figures we shall look at here, Kung is the most thoroughly secular—in the sense that he appears to be almost totally concerned with human life in its social and political setting. Thus there would be no point to a story of his going off into the wilderness to fight there against evil powers, or to encounter—or realize—a transcendent or supreme Reality (God, nirvana, etc). Kung is thoroughly concerned with mundane reality. Yet lest one get the impression from the last statement that he is rather dull, and indeed lest one carry away this wrong impression from his teaching, it is essential to remind ourselves what kind of a person he was. His own version: "I am a person who forgets to eat when he is enthusiastic about something, forgets all his worries in the enjoyment of it, and is not aware that old age is coming on" (*Analects*, 7.18).

How often do we become so absorbed in our work or leisure that we forget to eat? It is highly important for us to know that Kung could forget to eat. For many find Kung a little boring, a "square." His is a style that is rather out of vogue in the modern world—particularly in North America—much too stiff and formal. Most of us are impressed these days by easy informality. We believe in being nice to others, open, friendly. Even if we despise the naivety of the "ugly American," who cannot understand why others do not respond to his friendliness in the way the first-year psychology books and Norman Vincent Peale's "power of positive thinking" told him they would—nevertheless most of us live by a modified form of this style. We smile like the buttons not long ago in vogue; we are generally friendly—to anybody; we do not much like formal rituals.

Master Kung, on the other hand, is the great ritualist; there is a stiffness about him that puts many persons off.

But if stiffness and formality are one's dominant impression of Kung, I think one misunderstands him—and that is why it is so important to hear this first: he forgets to eat! A rare kind of enthusiasm! A more genuine enthusiasm than much of the hoopla of our enthusiastic society.

To this story should be added another. Kung one day asked some of his disciples (rarely recognized by rulers, it must be remembered!), "If a ruler were to recognize your worth and give you whatever you wanted, what would you ask for?" One student said, "Give me a kingdom hemmed in on all sides, I would make it brave." A second said, "Give me a district and in three years I would make it flourishing." A third said, "I would like to engage in the ceremonies of the ancestral temple and wear the ceremonial cap and gown." Thus spoke military, political, and liturgical experts! But the fourth said:

"In the latter days of spring, when the light spring garments are made, I would like to take along five or six grownups and six or seven youths to bathe in the River Yi, and after the bath go to enjoy the breeze in the woods among the altars of Wu-yi, and then return home loitering and singing on our way." Confucius heaved a deep sigh and said: "You are the man after my own heart" [deBary, 21].

You might be president or prime minister, but there is still nothing better than a hay ride or a country dance!

Keeping this kind of picture in the back of our minds, let us look at what are regarded as more central aspects of Confucian teaching.

The stimulus for Kung's teaching was a disintegrating society. The great Chou dynasty, which had been established about three hundred years before the time of Kung, was gradually falling apart. What was one to do about it? Kung's answer was a return to virtue, the virtue that had been characteristic of the ancients. When Kung said in the *Analects* (7.1) that he considered himself the oldest man who ever lived, he was emphasizing that he felt at home with the ancient traditions rather than with the contemporary disintegration.

China as a civilization was by this time quite old. The five Confucian classics (*I Ching*, "the book of changes"; *Shu Ching*, "the book of history"; *Shih Ching*, "the book of odes"; *Li Chi*, "the book of rites"; and *Chun-chiu*, the "spring and autumn annals") were probably all in existence, though not in as full a form as has come down to us; there is considerable evidence that they were all reworked and finally codified in the second or first century B.C. These books included traditional histories of the ancient sage kings who had ruled China around 2000 B.C. The Chinese looked back to this time as a golden age, a period of pristine perfection.

The idea of a golden age in the remote past is one that is very widespread in the religious history of humankind. Both Indians and Greeks, for example, developed the idea of four ages of history, the first of which was a golden age, and later ages progressively less noble, an indication of a deterioration in virtue. The uses of the golden age idea have also differed greatly. Hindus have concentrated upon the idea that we now live in Kali Yuga, the fourth and worst age, and much Hindu religious practice has been predicated upon the needs for these troubled times. Christians have often placed the golden age in the paradise of the garden of Eden, and have then correlated such paradisal conditions with a return of the Messiah; many Christian groups have exhibited an inordinate interest in the second coming of Christ, when Edenic perfection will be restored.

In China, Kung and other thinkers of his time used the golden age as a model. Each came up with their own picture of what the golden age was like. It is clear that from the ancient materials many different pictures could be drawn. But what is initially important is that Kung and the others had an essentially conservative stand. Their aim was to conserve, and indeed revive, the ancient virtue.

Thus Kung regarded himself as a transmitter. In his own opinion he was not original. He instructed his disciples in the ancient classics. Scholars looking at what he did, however, are convinced that he was indeed highly original. For what he did was to put together a system and to develop concepts on the basis of which the ancient perfection could be restored. We might say, to borrow a term from recent Canadian politics, that Kung was a "progressive conservative."

The center of his concern was humankind in its social and political context. In the *Analects* 18.6 he emphasizes that the human situation is radically different from that of the animal kingdom. There is already in the *Analects* indication of debate between Confucianists and Taoists (the latter we shall look at later). The Taoists concentrated upon the idea of harmony with nature as the essence of Tao, the way. Kung is pictured as countering this view with the assertion that the way, Tao, for humans has to be worked out in a form appropriate to the human situation. And what he is concerned about is a society that works fruitfully and harmoniously.

Kung was thus intensely practical. It is for this reason that he is pictured in the *Analects* 11.11 as not really interested in questions that people love to ask about ghosts and spirits and death. That he was unwilling to get into discussion of these matters has been used by some as evidence that Kung was not really religious. Whether that is true or not depends upon how one looks at religion. Does religion have essentially to do with the supernatural, the weird, the strange? Are sociology and politics divorced from religion?

Some might decide on the basis of modern Western society that they are, but a wider look at human history, even at quite recent events such as those in Iran, is sufficient to give one pause.

If one says that religion has to do with God, then the case of the Buddha may be more problematic than that of Kung: as Howard Smith has pointed out, Tien, heaven, holds an important place in Kung's thought. He refers to the Tao, the way he is setting forth, as the way of heaven. It is not clear how he conceived of heaven, and the conception itself does not appear to have been of importance to him. For again we notice that the center of his interests was the way of heaven *for human beings*.

If one says that religion has to do with rituals, then Kung was religious: as we shall see, he was very much interested in rituals. The question of what religion is about, however, is a very tricky one. The term is one that originated in ancient Rome, was developed in a Christian context, but was then used by Westerners to talk about phenomena in other cultures that appear analogous to what the Christian church in its ramifications is for Christians (see Smith, 19–49). A wide exposure to and study of the Christian church and its analogues leads me to suggest that the religious is best thought of as that dimension in which humans explore values, relate themselves to what they come to understand as the real, or the "really real," the truly significant. If one sees religion in this way, the crucial thing to say about Kung is that his religious interest was directed toward finding, or refinding, the way for persons to live together in harmony. And in attempting to do this, Kung undertook two different tasks. He first analyzed the structures of society; he then developed concepts, the practical application of which would infuse those structures with viability and humanity.

The claim by Kung in the *Analects* 18.6, that he must be a "man among other men"—perhaps we should now translate it as "a human among other human beings"—points to the first step in analysis—what has usually been referred to as the Rectification of Names. This has been defined as "that which makes the thing to which the name is applied *be* that thing and not something else." This needs further explanation. What Kung was concerned about was that persons should be in reality what they claim to be in title. He attempted to justify the existence of a range of positions in society, defining carefully what the essential nature and function of those positions are, and then to get persons to live truly in the context of their own positions. If it was important for a man to live as a man, it was also important for a king to be a king, a father to be a father, and so on:

> Duke Ching of Chi asked Master Kung about government. Master Kung replied saying, "Let the prince be a prince, the minister a minister, the father a father, and the son a son." The Duke said, "How true! For indeed where the prince is not a prince, the minister not a minister, the father not a father, the son not a son, one may have a dish of millet in front of one and yet not know if one will live to eat it" [Waley, *Analects*, 166].

One might say that the name represents for Kung a kind of Platonic ideal. Yet it is certainly not a supramundane ideal of which mundane reality can be only a pale reflection. Such would be a much too impractical approach for Kung. Rather the ideal is something that can be and should be lived.

A kind of subsection of the Rectification of Names is the idea of the Five Relationships. Human society is here analyzed into five basic significant relationships—those between ruler and subject, father and son, elder brother and younger brother, husband and wife, and friend and friend. In only one of these—the last—is it possible for Confucians to think in terms of equality of the partners in the relationship. The others each consist of a superior and an inferior. For the Confucian approach is strictly hierarchical. In each case it is the duty of the superior member to be protective, the duty of the inferior to be serving—all of which goes rather against the grain for modern liberal intellectuals for whom equality is axiomatic. One may find it less problematic if one realizes that Kung infuses the relationship with a spirit that makes terms such as "superior" and "inferior" inappropriate. Kung renders complementarity the key point of all the relationships. And although that does not make it any less a hierarchical system—indeed, for Kung the maintaining of the hierarchies is essential to the producing of a stable and harmonious society—it does make it possible for us who come with a very different perspective to hear the important things that Kung has to say.[36]

In attempting to understand the basis of this harmonious complementarity, the place to begin is *hsiao*, "filial piety." One might say that the whole Confucian system is built upon this. And the basis of filial piety is an ancient tradition of three years' mourning for one's parents, in which the chief mourner led a separate life, with special clothes and food, abstained from physical pleasures, and retired from public life:

> This mourning dress consists of an untrimmed sackcloth coat and skirt, fillets of the female nettle hemp, a staff, a twisted girdle, a hat whose hat-string is of cord, and rush shoes. The principal mourner lives in a booth built of branches leant against the house. He sleeps on straw and pillows, his head on a clod.
>
> He wails day and night, with no set times.
>
> For food he sups up congee, made twice a day, morning and evening, with one handful of grain.
>
> He does not put off the head or waist fillet when he sleeps. After the sacrifices of repose, he cuts a hole in the side of the booth and fits lintel and door-posts to it. He lays a mat over the straw, and sleeps on this. For food he eats coarse rice, and has water for his drinking. He wails once in the morning and once at night only.
>
> When he assumes the raw-silk hat, at the end of the first year of mourning, he lodges in a structure called the "outer sleeping apartment," and eats for the first time vegetables and fruit, partaking also of his ordinary food. No definite times are then prescribed for his wailing [Thompson, 49].

Why this system was developed nobody knows. It may have been related to a fear, observable among many peoples, of contamination by the dead, so that those who had been in contact with death had to go through a period of "disinfection." Or it may have been a fear that if the dead are not given proper attention, they will come back to haunt the living. But a more "rational" explanation could be given and Kung gives one:

> Tsai Wo asked about the three-year mourning [his opinion being that] one year was already long enough. "If the True

Gentlemen do not for three years carry on the practices of *li*, then *li* will certainly be harmed by this; if for three years they do not perform music, then music will certainly be lost. [In the space of a year] the old crops of grain are already no more, and the new grain has come up. . . . After one year [the mourning] might be ended."

The Master said, "To eat fine rice, and to wear brocaded silk—would you feel comfortable doing [these things after one year]?"

[Tsai Wo] said, "I would."

The Master said, "If you would feel comfortable, then do them. But the True Gentlemen, while in mourning, cannot relish the taste of his food, cannot enjoy the sound of music, cannot feel comfortable in his place—therefore he does not do [these things]. Now if you would feel comfortable, then do them."

When Tsai Wo had left, the Master said, "Yü [Tsai Wo's personal name] is really heartless. Only after a child is three years old does it leave its parents' arms; and [thus it is that] the three-year mourning is observed everywhere under Heaven. Didn't Yü [himself] have the three-year love of his parents?" [Thompson, 49–50].

In upholding the old system of mourning, Kung says that a true filial son *could* not be at ease in his ordinary clothes, at his usual tasks. If a man could be at ease, it would surely be a sign of hardheartedness.

This kind of reverence for deceased parents is, I think, unequalled in all the world. Three years' mourning seems to us excessively long, and highly inefficient. The other side of the coin is that it must have produced—or been produced by, or both—a very close-knit family system. In effect what Kung did was to focus on *hsiao* as the relationship appropriate to the family in which three years' mourning is the norm, emphasizing that the ritual is rightly the expression of that filial piety. So he makes the point (*Analects* 2.7) that the basis of family cohesion, the essence of filial piety, is not seen when a son cares for his parents' bodily needs—you do as much for domestic animals—but when there is also reverence.

Drawing on this picture of family cohesion, Kung goes on to

suggest that the way to stem the disintegration of society is to build it up so that it is the close-knit family system writ large; he thus extends the reciprocal caring of parents for children and children for parents into all of the five relationships: "Let a father be a father, a son a son, a ruler a ruler, a subject a subject. . . ."

More body is given to this building of a harmonious society in other concepts Kung developed. The most general is *shih*, "reciprocity." This is presented by Kung in the Golden Rule, in its negative version, "Do not do to others what you would not like yourself." (Kung also gave, somewhat less succinctly, the positive version.) This is the most general rule that could be applied at any time. But it is too unspecific to give strong direction for all interaction within society. So Kung goes further. By means of two concepts—*jen* and *li*—he portrays the lifestyle appropriate to a harmonious society. *Jen*, translated variously as "love," "human-heartedness," or "goodness," is portrayed as an inner quality of the heart that integrates the inner personality, gives serenity and poise. It incorporates the five virtues of courtesy, magnanimity, good faith, diligence, and kindness. It should be emphasized that Kung did not mean by *jen* any type of indiscriminate love. There is an appropriate context for this inner quality to be expressed and that is the context of the five relationships. To try to love universally, as a later Chinese sage, Mo-tzu, suggested, would have seemed to Kung as it did to his followers quite impractical, and even destructive of filial piety.

Li, like *jen*, is difficult to translate adequately, and again there have been many attempts—"ritual," "decorum," "etiquette," "propriety," the "ensemble of customs that govern all relationships." Within the context of contemporary North America it could cover everything from a solemn high Mass in the Roman Catholic Church, through pledging "allegiance to the flag of the United States of America," down to saying "Bless you!" when somebody sneezes.

For the successful running of society Kung saw the necessity of both inner virtue and appropriate outward expression. It is important to see that Kung's rationale for rituals was basically sociological. Appropriate rituals are necessary for the smooth running of society. A later scholar in the Confucian tradition, Hsun-tzu, gave a psychological rationale for rituals. Unlike

Freud, who tended to see rituals as a kind of collective neurosis, Hsun-tzu saw them as necessary vehicles for the expression of significant human emotions:

> Now the rites used on the occasion of birth are to embellish joy, those used on the occasion of death are to embellish sorrow, those used at sacrifice are to embellish reverence, those used on military occasions are to embellish dignity. In this respect the rites of all kings are alike, antiquity and the present age agree, and no one knows whence they came. . . .
>
> Sacrifice is to express a person's feeling of remembrance and longing, for grief and affliction cannot be kept out of one's consciousness all the time. When men are enjoying the pleasure of good company, a loyal minister or a filial son may feel grief and affliction. Once such feelings arise, he is greatly excited and moved. If such feelings are not given proper expression, then his emotions and memories are disappointed and not satisfied, and the appropriate rite is lacking [deBary, 110].

To return to Kung, it should be noted then that *li* is indispensable to *jen*. Without an appropriate ritual vehicle, the virtues become something different from what they really are (see *Analects* 8.2). To put things slightly differently, Kung has no place for the person who has a heart of gold and a rude exterior—no place for a rough diamond. For a harmonious society the precious jewel must have polish.

But rituals alone are also quite inappropriate. If Kung has no place for the boor, he also has no place for the fop. Ritual must be more than jade and silk; music is more than bell and drum (*Analects* 17.11).

Some years ago I visited the palace of Versailles. I had never seen a building so gorgeous. I wandered from one room to another continually amazed by each new magnificence. But after a time I found the magnificence and beauty depressing. I began to wonder why. In retrospect I find Kung of greatest help in understanding why I was finally so dissatisfied. Versailles is to me the perfect picture of *li* without *jen*. The building is a beautiful shell devoid of the inner virtue necessary for it to be truly and authentically human.

The person who combines the reciprocal virtues of *jen* and *li* Kung called *chun-tzu,* the "gentleman," the "superior person." Originally the term had been applied to those born to the hereditary nobility; Kung redefined the term so that a nobleman is not one who is born to the nobility but one who shows himself a person of nobility, who follows the way of nobility. Of general characteristics of the gentleman, Kung gives many details; his movements are free from violence and arrogance, his facial expressions are characterized by openness and sincerity, his speech free from coarseness, vulgarity, and impropriety; he does not talk too much, does not boast or push himself forward to display his superiority; he is moderate in conduct and opinion, avoids extremes, is never fanatical. In contrast with an inferior, the gentleman is calm and at ease, not worried or full of distress; cherishes virtue and not possessions; thinks of duties and not of personal favors; makes demands on himself rather than on others; is broad-minded rather than partisan; respects the teaching of the sages (whereas the inferior man scoffs at them).

But above all, according to *Analects* 10.9, "He must not sit on a mat that is not straight." Startling, yet the epitome of Kung's teaching—startling in its ability to jar us into thinking about the dominant values of our society. What would our society look like if we took Kung seriously on this? What would Kung say if he were to come into a modern university classroom after a lecture and see it scattered with cans and candy wrappings, student newspapers and professorial handouts—and chairs an erratic mess! What would he deduce about the quality of life in the modern city—New York?—exciting, barren, dangerous, dirty, decrepit.

I am certain that our society could benefit beyond measure if we were to explore thoroughly and draw on the wisdom of Kung's peculiar combination of enthusiasm and order: "He forgets to eat!" "He will not sit on a mat that is not straight!"

TEN SAYINGS FROM THE *TAO TE CHING*

1. *The Tao [Way] that can be told of*
   Is not the eternal Tao;

The name that can be named
Is not the eternal name.
Nameless, it is the origin of Heaven and earth;
Nameable, it is the mother of all things.

Always nonexistent,
That we may apprehend its inner secret;
Always existent,
That we may discern its outer manifestations.
These two are the same;
Only as they manifest themselves they receive different
names.

10. In loving the people and governing the land,
Can you practice nonaction (wu-wei)?
In opening and shutting the gates of Heaven,
Can you play the part of the female?

17. The best [government] is that whose existence only is known
by the people. The next is that which is loved and praised.
The next is that which is despised. . . .

18. It was when the Great Tao declined,
That there appeared humanity and righteousness.
It was when knowledge and intelligence arose,
That there appeared much hypocrisy.
It was when the six relations lost their harmony,
That there was talk of filial piety and paternal affection.
It was when the country fell into chaos and confusion,
That there was talk of loyalty and trustworthiness.

28. He who knows glory but keeps to disgrace,
Becomes the valley of the world.
Being the valley of the world,
He finds contentment in constant virtue,
He returns to the uncarved block.

The cutting up of the uncarved block results in vessels,
Which, in the hands of the sage, become officers.
Truly, "A great cutter does not cut."

32. *Tao is eternal, nameless. Though the uncarved block seems small, it may be subordinated to nothing in the world. If kings and barons can preserve it, all creation would of itself pay homage, Heaven and earth would unite to send sweet dew, and the people would of themselves achieve peace and harmony.*

   Once the block is cut, names appear. When names begin to appear, know then that there is a time to stop. It is by this knowledge that danger may be avoided.

37. *Tao invariably does nothing (wu-wei),*
   And yet there is nothing that is not done.

42. *Tao gave birth to One; One gave birth to Two; Two gave birth to Three; Three gave birth to all the myriad things. The myriad things carry the yin on their backs and hold the yang in their embrace, and derive their harmony from the permeation of these forces.*

   What others teach I also teach: "A man of violence will come to a violent end." This I shall regard as the parent of all teachings.

78. *Of all things yielding and weak in the world,*
   None is more so than water.
   But for attacking what is unyielding and strong,
   Nothing is superior to it,
   Nothing can take its place.

   That the weak overcomes the strong,
   And the yielding overcomes the unyielding,
   Everyone knows this,
   But no one can translate it into action.

80. *Let people revert to the practice of rope-knotting [instead of writing], and be contented with their food, pleased with their clothing, satisfied with their houses, and happy with their customs. Though there be a neighboring country in sight, and the people hear each other's cocks crowing and dogs barking, they would grow old and die without having anything to do with each other* [deBary, 51–62].

Master Lao

When we turn to Master Lao we find ourselves with respect to historicity in a situation a little like that with Krishna. The tradition is that the foundational text of the Taoists, the *Tao Te Ching*, was written by Master Lao. But it is not known if there ever was such a person. In contrast with Krishna, there is also very little detail developed about his life. He is the subject of quite a number of brief stories in Taoist tradition, but there is nothing of a connected narrative. The major features of his life story as accepted by tradition are that he was a contemporary of Master Kung, a government official who, in the unsettled conditions of the declining Chou dynasty, became disillusioned with the processes of government. He gradually developed something of a reputation for wisdom. It became quite widespread, for at the age of eighty-two he set off for Tibet on his water buffalo. At the border crossing he was recognized by the guard who prevailed upon him to write down some words of wisdom. Lao sat down and in a couple of days scribbled off the *Tao Te Ching*, a short text of eighty-one verses; then he mounted his water buffalo, moved off to Tibet, and was never seen again.

Brief though this is, it is quite significant. Neither Master Kung nor Master Lao are portrayed as going off into the wilderness like Gautama and then later returning to ordinary life. Kung's interest is thoroughly secular and concentrated on society, and thus the events of his life story are precisely there, in society. Lao's story on the other hand is centered in the journey away from society. He never returns as the Buddha does; instead he disappears into the landscape. And that is thoroughly in keeping with the Taoist vision of how life should be lived.

The *Tao Te Ching* is the most translated of all Chinese texts. No doubt this is related to the fact that it is so short. But it is also related, I think, to the fact that there are many versions of what various words and phrases mean. One can get some idea of the kinds of variations possible by comparing verse 1 above (pp. 82–83) with the following two versions, the first of which is by Arthur Waley and the second by Witter Bynner:

The Way that can be told of is not an Unvarying Way;
The names that can be named are not unvarying names.

It was from the Nameless that Heaven and Earth sprang;
The named is but the mother that rears the ten thousand
    creatures, each after its kind.
Truly, "Only he that rids himself forever of desire can see
    the Secret Essences;"
He that has never rid himself of desire can see only the
    Outcomes.
These two things issued from the same mould, but neverthe-
    less are different in name.
This "same mould" we can but call the Mystery,
Or rather the "Darker than any Mystery,"
The Doorway whence issued all Secret Essences

[Waley, *Way,* 141].

Existence is beyond the power of words
To define:
Terms may be used
But are none of them absolute.
In the beginning of heaven and earth there were no words,
Words came out of the womb of matter;
And whether a man dispassionately
Sees to the core of life
Or passionately
Sees the surface,
The core and the surface
Are essentially the same,
Words making them seem different
Only to express appearance.
If name be needed, wonder names them both:
From wonder into wonder
Existence opens [Bynner, 25].

Of these three versions it is clear that the Waley rendition has
attempted to be the most literal; but it is somewhat opaque. The
version on pages 82–83, above, has incorporated a particular interpretation without straying too far from the key words of the
original. Bynner in a finely poetic style gives the purport of the
piece, but the terminology is so far from the other two that it is
obvious that he has attempted to free himself of the Chinese con-

text and to speak in terms familiar to a Westerner. Hence, for example, the replacement of "Tao" by "existence."

All of which is to say that one will continually fear that one may be misunderstanding or distorting the text. Still, an attempt to picture Lao's views must be made.

The beginning and end and all of Lao's eighty-one verses is Tao. I was tempted to write of Lao's "system," but at least in the sense of system as something ordered, systematic, the word is quite inappropriate. Lao's thought reflects the universe as he understands it. It is systemic but not systematic. It is a flow, not a structure.

Tao is the all-encompassing reality. It cannot be conceived or defined. It is the mystery of mysteries. Those who know the reality of Tao do not speak about it; those who speak do not know it. If you must speak, you speak in paradoxes: nameless/nameable; nonexistent/existent. If you try to explain this you might say that ultimately it is beyond everything to which names might apply; if you think of the context in which names apply, the universe as we experience it, you might say it is "the way," Tao; or you might call it "mother," the origin of the whole natural world. If you think of existents, things that exist, Tao certainly does not exist; though you might say that it exists in the sense that existents are its outer manifestation.

If one comes to this from India, one might be tempted to see Tao as an equivalent of Brahman, which is there generally understood as the Ultimate Reality behind the instability and flow of the universe; the origin of it, the essence of it, the all of it. When you penetrate to it, when you "realize" Brahman, there is only Brahman, and the reality of the universe in its multiplicity is understood to be an illusion, a magician's show, a mirage (see, e.g., Zimmer, 418 ff.).

There is, however, a vastly different perspective to Indian views about Brahman and Taoist views of Tao. For Hindus generally, the flow of the universe is in the last analysis thought of in negative terms as bondage; Brahman is that which is stable and abiding, *beyond* the flow. For Taoists, Tao is the flowing of the flow. For Hindus the realization of Brahman is related experientially to the stillness of deep meditation. For Taoists the practical implications of Tao are that one flows with the flow. A corollary of this difference is that although at one level one could say of Brahman that it is nonexistent in the sense that it does not exist like other things, at another higher level it is the only existent, for it is the only reality; whereas for Tao there is more point to saying that apart from the existents in which it exists, it is non-existent. For Tao is not a transcendent reality, is not a reality *beyond* the phenomenon of the universe. Tao is the way of the universe in its continuous onward flow.

There are a number of images used to speak about Tao that elucidate this latter point. Tao is referred to as the mother (*Tao Te Ching*, 1.25), which suggests Tao as the origin of all; but another dimension of this image is suggested by related images: playing the part of the female, the space in a bowl, the hole in the center of a wheel, the valley. Two different but related ways of thinking about Tao are given here. The space in the bowl is the emptiness that is not the bowl, but without it the bowl is no bowl; the hole in the wheel is not the wheel, yet without it the wheel is no wheel. Creative emptiness! Creative nothing! The hole and the space are nothing, yet they are the most important part of the wheel and bowl, respectively. The images of female and valley suggest also for the image of the mother a quality of receptivity and yielding. And there is another image, in verse 78, which extends the understanding of this view of Tao—water. Water adapts itself to its surroundings. There is nothing more yielding than water, nothing more accommodating, nothing weaker. But it is exceedingly powerful. It bears, it buoys, it wears away rock, wears it smooth.

Verse 37 introduces an important term for understanding Tao: *wu-wei*. This has often been translated "nonaction," but many scholars have found that inadequate. Another suggested translation is "creative quietude." Perhaps there is no adequate translation per se, for the idea suggests (when it is applied to human life) spontaneous, natural behavior. "Tao invariably does nothing, and yet there is nothing that is not done," interpreted with the help of the above images, means that the activity of the Tao is everything, yet you do not see it acting, you are totally unaware of its achieving. You do not see the Tao fussing about doing things. Its acting is totally indistinguishable from the phenomena through which it acts.

There is a practical application of this. As I have already indicated, *wu-wei* is a concept that is applied to human life. For like Kung, Lao is interested in finding an appropriate way for creating a harmonious society. His version of how this is done is centered on *wu-wei*. "In loving the people and governing the land / can you practice *wu-wei*?"(v. 10). If the worst kind of government is one that is despised, the best is not one that is praised and loved, but one whose existence is just known, *barely* known. You do not praise the hole in the wheel; you are barely aware of its existence. You do not see Tao, let alone praise it. The best government is one that is so natural and spontaneous that one hardly knows that it is there.

And the kind of life that the people live is also to be characterized by *wu-wei* if the government is to be like that described. The characteristic lifestyle that the *Tao Te Ching* presents is the spontaneous, natural, yielding behavior of Tao. This is set over against the virtues developed by Kung (v. 18). Indeed Lao-tzu sees these virtues as symptoms, evidence of a kind of fall, a movement away from Tao. Lao's answer to the problems of society, as both he and Kung are experiencing them, is not a series of virtues but a return to Tao. (And this is not just to say that the ruler and people act in a manner that resembles the spontaneous flow of Tao. Rather one becomes in harmony with the flow, one allows the Tao to act in and through oneself.)

The idea of a falling away from the natural as the source of disharmony is expressed under another powerful image—that of the uncarved block. Lao calls for a return to the uncarved block (v. 28). If kings and barons can preserve the uncarved block, the people of itself will achieve harmony (v. 32). The cutting of the block results in names; when names appear, it is time to stop. To reinterpret: one may think that the great sculptor is one who can take a piece of wood or stone and chip or cut from it the figure of a man or a horse or whatever in a style that is vivid and striking. On the contrary, says Lao, a great sculptor does not cut. To cut is to limit. The uncarved block has boundless potential; the carved block is limited and limiting. Back to the boundless potential of the natural, or harmony with Tao!

What does he mean? There are suggestions that he wants a return to ignorance. He says that the ancient sage kings—he also, like Kung, sees himself as presenting the way of the ancients—

kept the people in ignorance. He suggests that the people should return to the practice of rope-knotting instead of writing; if they did, contentment would return, trouble and unrest would disappear (v. 80). But how seriously should one take this? It is, to say the least, surprising that the writer of such a work as the *Tao Te Ching*, replete with such sophisticated conceptualization, should suggest a return to ignorance.

I am inclined to think that one misses the point if one takes him literally here. His point, I think, is that knowledge and hypocrisy go hand in hand; chaos and confusion lead to talk of loyalty and trustworthiness (v. 18). The kind of interdependence of virtues and trouble that Lao-tzu sees is portrayed very vividly by Chuang-tzu, another Taoist whose work probably postdates the *Tao Te Ching*:

> The invention
> Of weights and measures
> Makes robbery easier.
> Signing contracts, setting seals,
> Makes robbery more sure.
> Teaching love and duty
> Provides a fitting language
> With which to prove that robbery
> Is really for the general good.
> > A poor man must swing
> > For stealing a belt buckle
> > But if a rich man steals a whole state
> > He is acclaimed
> > As statesman of the year.
> Hence if you want to hear the very best speeches
> On love, duty, justice, etc.,
> Listen to statesmen.
> But when the creek dries up
> Nothing grows in the valley.
> When the mound is levelled
> The hollow next to it is filled.
> And when statesmen and lawyers
> And preachers of duty disappear
> There are no more robberies either
> And the world is at peace.

Moral: the more you pile up ethical principles
And duties and obligations
To bring everyone in line
The more you gather loot
For a thief like Khang.
By ethical argument
And moral principle
The greatest crimes are eventually shown
To have been necessary, and, in fact,
A signal benefit
To mankind [Merton, 68–69].

A slightly different approach from Chuang-tzu may elucidate further:

In the age when life on earth was full, no one paid any special attention to worthy men, nor did they single out the man of ability. Rulers were simply the highest branches on the tree, and the people were like deer in the woods. They were honest and righteous without realizing that they were "doing their duty." They loved each other and did not know that this was "love of neighbor." They deceived no one yet they did not know that they were "men to be trusted." They were reliable and did not know that this was "good faith." They lived freely together giving and taking, and did not know that they were generous. For this reason their deeds have not been narrated. They made no history [Merton, 76].

We can return to Lao-tzu to say that for the Taoists knowledge, writing, books, sages, history are all symptomatic of a decline from the full humanity that is found in harmony with Tao. Ignorance, rope-knotting, and not needing books or history are symbolic of a life of fulfilled innocence. (I use this term because, it seems to me, Lao may well have developed these ideas from observing the preliterate, ahistorical, fulfilled life of childhood innocence.)

What, then, does Lao-tzu mean? Does he see hope for human society in a return to a kind of animal state, to the harmony that animals have with their environment? And when Lao is pictured as going off to Tibet, does that mean that the best thing a sage can

do is leave it all, go and live out among trees and mountains, let
the people enter anarchy, and hence eventually arrive at a kind of
animal contentment?

There is a story of Chuang-tzu that might seem to confirm such
speculation:

Chuang Tzu with his bamboo pole
Was fishing in Pu river.

The Prince of Chu
Sent two vice-chancellors
With a formal document:
"We hereby appoint you
Prime Minister."

Chuang Tzu held his bamboo pole.
Still watching Pu river,
He said:
"I am told there is a sacred tortoise,
Offered and canonized
Three thousand years ago,
Venerated by the prince,
Wrapped in silk,
In a precious shrine
On an altar
In the Temple.
What do you think:
Is it better to give up one's life
And leave a sacred shell
As an object of cult
In a cloud of incense
Three thousand years,
Or better to live
As a plain turtle
Dragging its tail in the mud?"

"For the turtle," said the Vice-Chancellor,
"Better to live
And drag its tail in the mud!"

"Go home!" said Chuang Tzu.
"Leave me here
To drag my tail in the mud!" [Merton, 93–94].

But there is another very important story from Chuang-tzu that
may help to elucidate the thinking of Lao, and enable us to bring
together different parts into a whole:

Prince Wen Hui's cook
Was cutting up an ox.
Out went a hand,
Down went a shoulder,
He planted a foot,
He pressed with a knee,
The ox fell apart
With a whisper,
The bright cleaver murmured
Like a gentle wind.
Rhythm! Timing!
Like a sacred dance,
Like "The Mulberry Grove,"
Like ancient harmonies!

"Good work!" the Prince exclaimed,
"Your method is faultless!"
"Method?" said the cook
Laying aside his cleaver,
"What I follow is Tao
Beyond all methods!

"When I first began
To cut up oxen
I would see before me
The whole ox
All in one mass.

"After three years
I no longer saw this mass.
I saw the distinctions.

"But now, I see nothing
With the eye. My whole being
Apprehends.
My senses are idle. The spirit
Free to work without plan
Follows its own instinct
Guided by natural line,
By the secret opening, the hidden space,
My cleaver finds its own way.
I cut through no joint, chop no bone.

"A good cook needs a new chopper
Once a year—he cuts.
A poor cook needs a new one
Every month—he hacks!

"I have used this same cleaver
Nineteen years.
It has cut up
A thousand oxen
Its edge is as keen
As if newly sharpened.

"There are spaces in the joints;
The blade is thin and keen:
When this thinness
Finds that space
There is all the room you need!
It goes like a breeze!
Hence I have this cleaver nineteen years
As if newly sharpened!

"True, there are sometimes
Tough joints. I feel them coming,
I slow down, I watch closely,
Hold back, barely move the blade,
And whump! the part falls away
Landing like a clod of earth.

"Then I withdraw the blade,
I stand still
And let the joy of the work
Sink in.
I clean the blade
And put it away."

Prince Wan Hui said,
"This is it! My cook has shown me
How I ought to live
My own life!" [Merton, 45–47].

This seems to me like a midrash on the words in verse 28 of the *Tao Te Ching*: "A great cutter does not cut."[37] Prince Wan Hui's cook becomes a demonstration of how one should live. Not without knowledge, for clearly the cook has a profound knowledge of his ox. Much more profound than that of hackers. And it is clear that by hackers Chuang means the Confucian scholars. The peddling of virtues for the construction of a better society is, in the Taoist view, "hacking." Not the scholarly virtues, not the kind of thing you can write in books, but a skill that is so in harmony with the nature of the task that one does nothing at all—no aggression, no hacking, so that at the end of the task the blade of the knife is as good as the day it was bought. This is the Taoist ideal.

But what does that mean in practical terms? Again, the answer is not easy. Perhaps the best approach is to look at a Taoist painting. Most of them are scenes from nature. There are almost always persons there, but at first you do not see them. Look hard and you find them, down in one corner, or walking along a path. But the first impression is the important one—persons are lost in, perfectly blended into, the landscape. The Taoist ideal is not that humanity should dominate nature, not humans lording it over the beasts, but humanity in tune with nature, a minute part of the whole. The Taoist conception of *wu-wei* points to a life that is profoundly nonviolent. At the level of humanity itself, this is seen in the *Tao Te Ching* condemnation of violence (v. 42), and the judgment that soldiering is the worst occupation. At the level of the relationship between humanity and the natural world, it is seen in a highly sensitive approach to ecology.

All of this seems in deep contradiction with the Confucian view of how to live life. How then could people be both Confucian and Taoist? In practical terms what tended to happen was this. The Confucian tradition and its organization became intimately tied to family life and the state. The rituals related to the ancestors of the family and the rituals of the imperial family were Confucian. The Confucian philosophy also became the political philosophy, the basis on which the state was organized. The Taoist strand became related to more personal needs. It developed as a healing cult, and then beyond that into a way for obtaining immortality: through appropriate attention to the true needs of the body, in accordance with the Tao of the body, one could become immortal! (See Welch, 83–123). And beyond that there was developed a large "pantheon" of Boundless Immortals, humans who had managed to achieve immortality; and these then became helpers to whom mortals could turn in time of need. This development of the "Taoist Church" (Welch, 113), as it is often called, ran somewhat in parallel with the development of the Buddhist movement in China, for they vied with each other in offering immortality and superhuman helpers.

This was at the popular level. At the level of more sophisticated thought, such as we have been looking at, many variations were developed. Some Confucian scholars developed a Taoist cosmic frame for Confucian principles, arguing that the way of Kung is *the* way appropriate to human society (see deBary, chap. 8). Many intellectuals were centrally Confucianists—but when, as a result of Confucian overbureaucratization, things began to fall apart, then they took literally Lao's journey into Tibet, and Chuang's "dragging his tail in the mud," and went and lived in the forest, in harmony with nature (see Wright, 28–31, 44–45). And there were a few who did what I think is the most promising approach to bringing these extremes together: they acknowledged the practical need in human life for order, structure—the kind of thing offered by the Confucian virtues—but attempted to infuse them with the spirit of the Tao, a deeply intuitive awareness of the needs of human-nature-within-nature. But it is the opinion of many scholars that this "spirit of the Tao" found its most mature expression later in China and Japan largely in a branch of the Buddhist movement—in the sect called Chan in China and thence, in Japan, Zen; and then in a variety of facets of Chinese and Japanese life that are simple yet profound expressions of the natural and harmonious flow of things: Tai Chi and judo, the Japanese arts of archery, gardening, and flower arranging, and the tea ceremony (see Linssen, 187–213).[38]

The interplay of these two strands in Chinese society points to something to which I shall return in concluding this discussion—the fact that in the religious experience of humankind there seem to be two different focuses of religious interest: one like Kung's, the construction and maintenance of a viable society, harmonious, ordered, and just, the other, like Lao's, an experience on the one hand more individualistic, on the other more cosmic in scope.

Most of the major religious movements of the world combined these different aspects of religiousness into one path, one system; in China, they have often existed in interplay and this suggests a model that may be more appropriate to the times in which we live.

IV

BURNING BUSH AND MOUNTAIN CAVE: MOSES AND MUHAMMAD

THE DECALOGUE FROM THE BOOK OF EXODUS

God spoke, and these were his words:
I am the Lord your God who brought you out of Egypt, out of the land of slavery.
You shall have no other god to set against me.
You shall not make a carved image for yourself nor the likeness of anything in the heavens above, or on the earth below, or in the waters under the earth.
You shall not bow down to them or worship them; for I, the Lord your God, am a jealous god. I punish the children for the sins of the fathers to the third and fourth generations of those who hate me. But I keep faith with thousands, with those who love me and keep my commandments.
You shall not make wrong use of the name of the Lord your God; the Lord will not leave unpunished the man who misuses his name.
Remember to keep the sabbath day holy. You have six days to labour and do all your work. But the seventh day is a sabbath of the Lord your God; that day you shall not do any work, you, your son or your daughter, your slave or your slave-girl, your cattle or the alien within your gates; for in six days the Lord made

*heaven and earth, the sea, and all that is in them, and on the
seventh day he rested. Therefore the Lord blessed the sabbath day
and declared it holy.*

*Honour your father and your mother, that you may live long in
the land which the Lord your God is giving you.*

You shall not commit murder.

You shall not commit adultery.

You shall not steal.

You shall not give false evidence against your neighbour.

*You shall not covet your neighbour's house; you shall not covet
your neighbour's wife, his slave, his slave-girl, his ox, his ass, or
anything that belongs to him.*

(Exodus 20:2–17)

A History of Antagonisms

In view of recent events in the Near East, to put together in one
section Moses and Muhammad must appear overdaring. I do it in
part because I think it is exceedingly important for both Jews and
Muslims to realize how close Moses and Muhammad stand together. Quite apart from such interests, however, it is clear that if
one looks at the life stories of these key religious figures as modifications of the heroic cycle delineated by Joseph Campbell, then
Moses and Muhammad stand very close in the forms that they
portray. In addition, the systems that have been developed by
Jews and Muslims and that they attribute respectively to Moses
and Muhammad are also, in the structural forms that they take,
quite similar. A third respect in which they stand together, and
one that needs some investigation by the West, is the fact that
among Christians both have had a very bad press. This is no
doubt partly because Moses and Muhammad are the two great
rivals of Jesus as religious figures of Western history. But the
antagonism toward them from Christians runs very deep. Quite
recent "objective" Western historians have judged Muhammad
to be an epileptic or a highly immoral leader (Guillaume, 25), and
for centuries Moses was portrayed in Christian art with horns, a
symbolic portrayal of the evil Jew (Mellinkoff, 121–40).

The antagonism of Christians toward Moses and more generally toward Jews has been traced back as far as the New Testa-

ment, to the Gospel according to John. Here there is the well-known statement, "The law was given through Moses; grace and truth came through Jesus Christ." Few modern scholars of the Bible would want to maintain that that is an accurate portrayal of the relationship between these two figures. In addition, in John's Gospel the Jews are painted generically in a very negative light as those responsible for the death of Jesus.[39]

The full scale of Christian antagonism toward Jews, however, seems to have come only after there was antagonism on another front—toward the followers of Muhammad. It has been suggested that the antagonism of so-called objective historians, such as I have mentioned, to the person of Muhammad, is an extension of an antagonism felt very strongly by Christians toward the Islamic movement from the time of the Crusades—and less strongly before that. Within one hundred years of the founding of Islam, the name of Muhammad was repeated daily from Spain to Iran. It was only the victory of Charles Martel at the Battle of Tours in 732 that stopped the advance of Muslims into France. Martel pushed them back over the Pyrenees into Spain, which remained Islamic for several hundred years.

The threat to Europe from the Muslims reached another high point about seven hundred years later: Constantinople fell to the Turks in 1453, and they advanced up through Eastern Europe to Vienna. It was only there that they were finally stayed. In addition, for a large part of the thirteen hundred years since the time of Muhammad, Islamic civilization has been as successful and glorious as Christian civilization, if not more so. It is only in the last four hundred years that Europe has been clearly dominant; and now the tide may be turning again.

The power of Islam was not only military and cultural. Christianity suffered a defeat in a spiritual sense, in that millions of persons from Syria and Egypt, across North Africa and into Spain, were converted from the Christian church to Islam.

The antagonism came to a head in another form in that central event of the twelfth and thirteenth centuries, the Crusades, where the forces of the two rival movements fought for the control of the Holy Land and Jerusalem. The earliest serious persecutions of Jews by Christians in Europe came at the same time. As crusaders journeyed toward the Holy Land, they slaughtered Jews, first in the Rhineland and then in other parts of Europe.

One can understand, then, that the antagonism felt toward Jews and Muslims, toward Moses and Muhammad, brought them together in Christians' eyes. Moses was seen as, at best, a preparation for the gospel that was presented in Jesus, and his message was regarded as one that had been superseded. Those who continued to follow his path, those who remained staunchly as members of the Jewish community, the Jewish people, had, in Christian eyes, rejected the truth. Similarly, Muslims were seen as rejecting the truth and erring from the Christian way—apostates.

In view of past and continuing antagonisms, then, it is imperative that we look at these two figures in such a way that we can appreciate the depth of the religious heritage that is available for all humanity through them.

Moses and the Exodus

The first thing to note in the life of Moses is that its central event is also the central and determinative event of the people of Israel and of the Hebrew Bible—that of the exodus, the escape of the people of Israel from the land of Egypt. There is, as in the case of our other great founder figures, considerable detail about Moses' life before this time. In a motif that we find paralleled in the case of Jesus and Krishna, Moses' life is portrayed as being in great danger when he was just a baby. In each case the danger comes from a king—Herod in the case of Jesus, Kamsa in the case of Krishna, and the pharaoh, the king of Egypt in the case of Moses. In all three cases, the essential point is that they survived such threats. There was a protective power more able than the destructive one. In some respects, the survival of Moses is more triumphant than that of the others. The story of his being laid in the bullrushes, found by the king's daughter, and taken off to the palace of the king, there to grow up as part of Egyptian royalty is a massive reversal of the plan of the evil powers. The result is that, like the Buddha, Moses begins the determinative phase of his life, the heroic cycle, in a royal palace. Like the Buddha, he experiences a call that takes him into the wilderness. The nature of the call, however, is quite different from that of the Buddha: not the general condition of humankind but the quite specific degradation in which he finds his people, the people of Israel from whom he has come.[40]

The details of his going off into the wilderness are themselves interesting. He attempted to stand up against the brutal mistreatment of the Israelite slaves, in the process killing an Egyptian taskmaster, and as a result found himself profoundly mistrusted by the Israelites themselves. He does not know how to handle this and he flees. Out in the wilderness, he eventually joins up with some desert dwellers, marries a woman from a desert tribe, and then one day when he is caring for his father-in-law's sheep he encounters something that has a profound effect upon his life. Moses comes face to face with God via an experience of a bush that burns but is not consumed. The experience of Moses before the burning bush must surely be seen as a parallel to that of Gautama under the *bodhi* tree. The symbolism of the burning bush draws upon two important motifs. One is the tree that is significant in the case of Buddha. (It is also important in the case of Krishna who is portrayed as standing beneath a *kadamba* tree playing his flute, and in the case of Jesus who hangs on a tree.) The tree is a symbol of rebirth, a fitting portrayal of the revitalization of a person or a people by a transcendent power or a transcendent experience. The element of flame in the burning bush adds to the impression of vitality that the tree gives us. (The image of the flame continues to be important in Jewish and Christian thinking, so that when Christians portray the vitality of the day of Pentecost, a sudden bursting forth of new energy in the "baptism of the Spirit," this vitality is shown in the picture of flames of fire over the head of each person.)

In the burning bush Moses encounters God, the one whose name is "Yahweh"—at least this is what scholars now tend to accept as the name of God.[41] The word probably carries the implication given to Moses before the burning bush that God is "the One who truly is." (Thus, Exodus 3:14: "I AM; that is who I am.") This awesome experience constitutes for Moses a call to return to the land of Egypt to bring his people out of captivity, out of their slavery; and it is this that he manages to do after a long period of attempting to convince the Egyptian king that he should allow the enslaved people to go free. Impetus toward the freeing of the people is provided by a series of plagues experienced by the Egyptians. A final devastating event, in which the firstborn of every Egyptian household is slain, is interpreted by Moses as a further act of God, and the king consents to let the Israelites go.

The final stage of their movement out of Egypt comes at the point of the crossing of the Red—more correctly, it is now usually translated "Reed"—Sea. Here, according to the traditional picture, the king, having regretted that he had allowed the enslaved people to get away, sends his charioteers and soldiers after the Israelite community. Moses, raising his rod over the sea, enables the children of Israel to go through on dry land; when they have all passed through, the waters close again and the Egyptians are drowned. The song of Moses, as it is recorded in Exodus 15, portrays the event in poetic style:

> I will sing to the Lord for he has risen up in triumph;
> The horse and his rider he has hurled into the sea.
>> The Lord is my refuge and my defence,
>> he has shown himself my deliverer.
>> He is my God, and I will glorify him;
>> he is my father's God and I will exalt him.
>> The Lord is a warrior: the Lord is his name.
>> The chariots of Pharaoh and his army he has cast into the
>>> sea;
>> the flower of his officers
>> are engulfed in the Red Sea.
>> The watery abyss has covered them,
>> they sank into the depths like a stone.
> Thy right hand, O Lord, is majestic in strength:
> thy right hand, O Lord, shattered the enemy.
>> In the fullness of thy triumph
>> thou didst cast the rebels down:
>> thou didst let loose thy fury;
>> it consumed them like chaff [Exod. 15:1–7].

This clearly is a use of the other great motif of the hero story, drawn on by the accounts of these great religious figures—that of the battle. It is here, however, not as in the case of the Buddha, a prelude to the great heroic encounter with reality, but part of a separate journey. For whereas in the case of the Buddha there is one essential heroic journey, in the case of Moses there are two. Moses' own journey into the wilderness is followed by another in which he leads his people into the same wilderness. In one journey the central event is that of his encounter with God; in the other the central event is that of the battle against hostile forces.

This motif of the battle against evil powers is one that has considerable prehistory in both India and the Near East. In both cases there is in the earliest literature an account of a battle between a deity, a central and highly important deity, and a dragon-figure representing, it would appear, chaos—the chaos out of which the universe is created.[42] In India, it is the story of Indra and Vritra; in Mesopotamia, of Marduk and Tiamat. The conflict myth as it occurs at the beginning of the literary histories of India and Mesopotamia is a story of creation as an ordering of the universe. In later phases of the literature, in both India and the West, the opponents of the heroic figures often represent other negative experiences. In the case of this event, the exodus, the enemy represents not chaos but oppression. The central event of the exodus is an event of release from oppressive and binding forces. The black spiritual of the nineteenth century caught the theme very well: "Now let us all from bondage flee / And let us all in Christ be free."[43] (The last line, of course, reflects also the Christian heritage.)

The link between the account in Exodus of the overcoming of the forces of oppression and the early Mesopotamian creation story of Marduk and Tiamat, mentioned above, has been made more strongly by recent scholarly attempts to understand the event of the exodus. As scholars have examined in detail the account of this escape, they have concluded that there are perhaps three different stories compounded together in one continuous narrative. Evidence from within the narrative would suggest that according to one version a cloud came between the Israelites and the Egyptians, and thus the former were able to escape. According to another version, the Egyptians were crossing the sea in ships that sank in the waters, sank to the bottom of the sea. The third version is the one that has become the more embracing one—in that the other two are incorporated into it—the parting of the waters as Moses held out his rod, and the eventual closing of the waters over the Egyptians.

Most scholars accept that it is virtually impossible for us to know in detail what actually happened in the great escape from

Egypt. What appears to have happened in at least two of the versions is that the account of the freeing from oppression has been combined with a later version of the Marduk-Tiamat story deriving from an area that is now Lebanon, an account of the overcoming of the god Yam ("Sea") by the chief god of the Ugaritic pantheon, Baal (Cross, 125). Scholars think that this myth may have been taken over by those who presented the story of the exodus, and transformed it, so that the sea became something that God used to defeat evil forces. One should note a very important nuance here. In the story of Gautama, it is Gautama who is victorious over the forces of Mara, with the result that he becomes the Buddha. In the many battles of Krishna against demonic beings, the hidden agenda is that he is God in human form. In the case of the exodus, the distinction between Moses and God is radical. Thus, it is not Moses' battle but God's, not Moses' victory over oppressive forces, but God's. It is God who acts for the people of Israel.

This leads us to another feature of this version of the conflict myth: that it is a story of the *relationship* between God and God's people. The word that is central to this relationship is "covenant." This word referred to relationships between various states in the Middle East around this time. A large, powerful state would take under its wing smaller, less powerful states, and a pact, a binding oath, would be made between the two nations concerned. In the usual state of affairs, the stronger nation would bind itself to protect the weaker nation when necessary, and the weaker would pay some kind of tribute to the stronger for the protection thus offered.

In the portrayal of the relationship between God and the Israelites, this binding form took on a new dimension. Israel perceived that it was God who had done everything, that it was God who had taken the initiative. The people had been chosen to be God's own special people. As the prophet put it "the people who were no people have become God's people" (Hos. 2:23; cf. Rom. 8:25–26). This did not mean that the Israelites had no responsibilities—on the contrary they saw it as essential that they fulfill their part in the binding relationship. As Israel's theology developed, this binding relationship was seen as taking place in different stages, an earlier phase of the covenant relationship, with the patriarch Abraham, requiring of him a practice that continues to be carried on among Jews, the practice of circumcision. In the context of the exodus, the response of Israel is focused on the observance of the Sabbath day, a special day—every seventh day, set aside from other days, a day not for work but for contemplation of God and God's greatness. This practice, which like that of circumcision effectively set the Israelites off from others, represented to them their distinctiveness.

The picture of Israel as being distinctive, chosen by God as God's own people, has sometimes been used by anti-Semitic groups as a complaint against Jews—that they have some kind of superiority complex." The potentiality for such is undercut by the context that Jews themselves perceive in their chosenness. They see the act of God as purely God's act, something not dependent upon their goodness. The Jews of the biblical period are very much aware of the covenant love of God, the fact that they were brought into existence as God's people purely by divine grace. Not that they are unaware that this is a tremendous privilege. They accept it as such, but they are aware also that here there is a terrifying responsibility. It is a dreadful thing to fall into the hands of the living God.

The ambivalence that they have held about being this people chosen by God is portrayed in a typically wry story that Jews tell about how they came to be chosen. God, looking for a people to be God's own, went around to all the nations of the earth and asked each in turn to be that special people. God began with the large nations, the important ones, and each said no. Finally there was nobody left but an insignificant little group, the people of Israel, a people enslaved in Egypt. So God picked them; they being the last and the least significant could do little but say yes.

As has been said, the Israelites saw the fact that God had chosen them as a deep privilege and an awesome responsibility. They took very seriously their part in the covenant relationship. Their response was focused in the act of circumcision and in the practice of keeping a special holy day, a Sabbath day. But these are specific focuses of a broader response, the response best expressed in one word whose meaning we need to explore. The word is "Torah."

Torah literally means "teaching." When Jews later came to

codify their religious literature they grouped together the first five books of their Bible and referred to it all as Torah. But within those books there is a more central focus of this word. Much later, when Jews looked at the materials of these five books they divided them into two different kinds. One set of materials they called *halakhah,* a word that means "walking." The other set they called *haggadah,* meaning "narration."In *halakhah* they included the injunctions, the laws that God gave to the people, as tradition had it, through Moses. In *haggadah* they included everything else—stories, fables, accounts of creation, theological discussions about the nature of God, the history of the people. For Jews of this later period the center of Torah was *halakhah,* walking being a particularized image, with a considerable biblical heritage that stands for right action, see, e.g., Exod. 16:4; Ps. 84:11; Prov. 2:20.[45] For Jews, Torah is centrally about the way in which they should live their lives.

According to tradition, within these first five books there are 613 laws that God gave to Moses as injunctions for the life of the people. These 613 laws, the central focus of Torah, comprise quite diverse materials. There are some that have to do with what we would call ritual activity, others that we would regard as ethical, and there are some that have to do with what we would today focus in a court of law—civil and criminal law. The center of this law is the ten statements (given at the beginning of this chapter), the Decalogue, the Ten Commandments. Four of the commandments have to do with the relationship of the people with God, and six express in very basic terms relationships that should exist among the people itself.[46] Later Jews, Jesus among them, took two texts from different parts of Torah (Deut. 6:15 and Lev. 19:18) and combined them, seeing them together as a further concise summary of what Torah is about: "Love the Lord your God with all your heart, with all your soul, with all your strength, and with all your mind; and your neighbour as yourself" (Luke 10:27).

But Torah was not just a matter of easy generalizations about the relationship of the Israelites to God and to each other. The laws of Torah had to do with the life of a nation as well as what *we* might think of as specifically religious relationships. That is, there is in Torah no division of religious and secular—all is part of what God has given to this people, this nation. As a result, there are quite specific details about what should be done in particular problem situations of a society. For example:

> When a man steals an ox or sheep and slaughters or sells it, he shall repay five beasts for the ox and four for the sheep. He shall pay in full; if he has no means, he shall be sold to pay for the theft. But if the animal is found alive in his possession, be it an ox, ass, or sheep, he shall repay two. If a burglar is caught in the act and is fatally injured, it is not murder; but if he breaks in after sunrise and is fatally injured, then it is murder [Exod. 22:1–4].

These are somewhat obscure examples of the interest that is shown in such things as restitution for illegal acts, and the appropriate punishments for specific crimes. Torah is aimed at ensuring that the Israelites live together in harmony, in seeing that justice is done at the community level.

There are in the details of Torah some surprises—laws that have nothing to do with either ethics or legal restitution. There is, for example, this statement on what kinds of food may be eaten:

> The Lord spoke to Moses and Aaron and said, Speak to the Israelites in these words: Of all animals on land these are the creatures you may eat: you may eat any animal which has a parted foot or a cloven hoof and also chews the cud; those which have only a cloven hoof or only chew the cud you may not eat. These are: the camel, because it chews the cud but has not a cloven hoof; you shall regard it as unclean; the rock-badger, because it chews the cud but has not a parted foot; you shall regard it as unclean; the hare, because it chews the cud but has not a parted foot; you shall regard it as unclean; the pig, because it has a parted foot and a cloven hoof but does not chew the cud; you shall regard it as unclean. You shall not eat their flesh or even touch their dead bodies; you shall regard them as unclean. Of creatures that live in water these you may eat: all those that have fins and scales, whether in salt water or fresh; but all that have neither fins nor scales, whether in salt or fresh water, includ-

ing both small creatures in shoals and larger creatures, you shall regard as vermin. They shall be vermin to you; you shall not eat their flesh, and their dead bodies you shall treat as those of vermin. Every creature in the water that has neither fins nor scales shall be vermin to you [Lev. 11:1–12].

A number of different explanations have been given for these restrictions. The commonest one has referred them to hygiene. The suggestion is that the Israelites became aware that eating pork and shellfish in their climate led to severe illnesses, and so restrictions were made to provide healthy food for the people. This hardly seems sufficient, however, to explain the complexity of the system. Other writers have suggested that the basis on which these distinctions were made is purely arbitrary: all it entailed was a setting up of restrictions as a means whereby Israelites gained and maintained, each time they sat down to a meal, a strong sense of their identity—their identity as a different people. More recently there has been a suggestion that what is prescribed here is tied to a concept of the orders of creation: that the animals judged unclean, unfit for human consumption, are those that are in some sense hybrids, and perceived as not truly part of the order of creation as God originally established it. The implication of this would be that the people of Israel saw itself as a people wholly under God, and reminded itself powerfully of its relationship to God by the care that it took to ensure that its food was in line with what God had originally intended for the world. This explanation still sees these prohibitions as having to do with Israel's identity—but it sees the central point of that identity as the "holy" ("whole," "wholesome") people of God expressed in a powerful symbolism of food (see Douglas, 63–72).

These are part of an extensive set of regulations that determine what is "kosher," fit for use. Other notable practices involved the consumption of meat only when the animal had been killed according to strict ritual patterns, and a prohibition against the boiling of a kid in its mother's milk, which came to be expanded as a prohibition against the mixing of milk dishes and meat dishes.

Many of the prohibitions and injunctions reveal an interest in ritual cleanliness. There is a strong aversion to bodily discharges, so that discharges of menstrual blood or of semen render a person polluted. There are regulations indicating the means whereby such polluted persons may regain their purity.

Even those scholars who accept that there was a "historical Moses" regard it as highly unlikely that he was responsible for all these laws, or even any more than a handful of them. But when Jews looked back on the events of their history, they related these injunctions to the foundations of their history, to the primal covenant act of God in the exodus. Torah was their response to God's covenant love.

In emphasizing the exodus as central, there is a further aspect of importance to my train of thought. It is generally accepted by scholars that much of what is recorded about what went on before the period of the exodus, back to the patriarch Abraham, is told in such a way that it looks forward to the exodus. Thus the emphasis on Abraham's moving out into the unknown at the call of God and under divine guidance (Gen. 11) toward the land of Canaan is a prefiguring of the exodus event. Furthermore, scholars see the conception of God as responsible for the creation as also something developed from an *earlier* view of God's activity in the exodus events. That is, although in the Bible as it has come down to us everything begins with the creation, it is almost certainly the exodus event that was primary in the experience of Israel. From contemplating this event—it may have taken five hundred years—their thinkers came to a realization that the One who had acted in the events of history to release them from slavery was the Lord of all history and the Lord of all creation.[47]

I am saying, then, that the hero cycle has been modified in the case of Moses by the perception of how life should be lived, that the second journey is added in such a way as to emphasize as powerfully as possible the corporate nature of the relationship between God and the people. The event of the burning bush, although set at the beginning of the crucial elements of the story, is nevertheless not the most important. Moses' personal experience has no real significance per se. What is important is what happened as a result of this call: the liberation of the people from slavery, the bringing of a slave people into a relationship with God, and the grand structure of Torah as the basis on which the people is to live.[48]

And a similar emphasis applies also in the case of Muhammad—to whom we now turn.

TEN WORDS FROM THE QURAN

Fixed is the Day of Judgment. On that day the Trumpet shall be sounded and you shall come in multitudes. The gates of heaven shall be flung open and the mountains shall pass away and become like vapour.

Hell will lie in ambush, a home for the transgressors. There they shall abide long ages: there they shall taste neither refreshment nor any drink, save boiling water and decaying filth: a fitting recompense. They disbelieved in Our reckoning and roundly denied Our revelations. But We counted all their doings and wrote them down. We shall say:"Taste this: you shall have nothing but mounting torment!"

As for the righteous, they shall surely triumph. Theirs shall be gardens and vineyards, and high-bosomed maidens for companions: a truly overflowing cup.

There they shall hear no idle talk nor any falsehood. Such is the recompense of your Lord—a gift that shall suffice them: the Lord of the heavens and the earth and all that lies between them; the Merciful, with whom no one can speak.

On the day when the Spirit and the angels stand up in their ranks, they shall not speak; except him who shall receive the sanction of the Merciful and declare what is right.

That day is sure to come. Let him who will, seek a way back to his Lord. We have forewarned you of an imminent scourge: the day when man will look upon his works and the unbeliever cries: "Would that I were dust!"

(78.17–40)

Righteousness does not consist in whether you face towards the east or the west. The righteous man is he who believes in Allah and the Last Day, in the angels and the Scriptures and the prophets; who for the love of Allah gives his wealth to his kinsfolk, to the orphans, to the needy, to the wayfarers and to the beggars, and for the redemption of captives; who attends to his prayers and pays the alms-tax; who is true to his promises and steadfast in trial and adversity and in times of war. Such are the true believers; such are the God-fearing.

(2.177)

Believers, retaliation is decreed for you in bloodshed: a free man for a free man, a slave for a slave, and a female for a female. He who is pardoned by his aggrieved brother shall be prosecuted according to usage and shall pay him a liberal fine. This is a merciful dispensation from your Lord. He that transgresses thereafter shall be sternly punished.

Men of understanding! In retaliation you have a safeguard for your lives; perchance you will guard yourselves against evil.

(2.178–79)

Believers, fasting is decreed for you as it was decreed for those before you: perchance you will guard yourselves against evil. Fast a certain number of days, but if any one of you is ill or on a journey let him fast a similar number of days later on; and for those that can afford it there is a ransom: the feeding of a poor man. He that does good of his own accord shall be well rewarded; but to fast is better for you, if you but knew it.

In the month of Ramadhan the Koran was revealed, a book of guidance with proofs of guidance distinguishing right from wrong. Therefore, whoever of you is present in that month let him fast.

(2.183–85)

Make the pilgrimage and visit the Sacred House for His sake. If you cannot, send such offerings as you can afford and do not shave your heads until the offerings have reached their destination. But if any of you is ill or suffers from an ailment of the head, he must pay a ransom either by fasting or by alms-giving or by offering a sacrifice. . . .

Make the pilgrimage in the appointed months. He that intends to perform it in those months must abstain from sexual intercourse, obscene language, and acrimonious disputes while on pilgrimage. Allah is aware of whatever good you do. Provide yourselves well: the best provision is piety. Fear Me, then, you that are endowed with understanding.

(2.196–97)

Men have authority over women because Allah has made the one superior to the other, and because they spend their wealth to maintain them. Good women are obedient. They guard their unseen parts because Allah has guarded them. As for those from whom you fear disobedience, admonish them and send them to beds apart and beat them. Then if they obey you take no further action against them. Allah is high, supreme.

(4.35)

Fight for the sake of Allah those that fight against you, but do not attack them first. Allah does not love the aggressors.

Kill them wherever you find them. Drive them out of the places from which they drove you. Idolatry is worse than carnage. But do not fight them within the precincts of the Holy Mosque unless they attack you there; if they attack you put them to the sword. Thus shall the unbelievers be rewarded: but if they mend their ways, know that Allah is forgiving and merciful.

Fight against them until idolatry is no more and Allah's religion reigns supreme. But if they mend their ways, fight none except the evil-doers.

(2.190–92)

Believers, eat of the wholesome things with which We have provided you and give thanks to Allah, if it is He whom you worship.

He has forbidden you the flesh of animals that die a natural death, blood, and pig's meat; also any flesh that is consecrated in the name of any other than Allah. But whoever is constrained to eat any of these, through neither appetite nor wilful sin, incurs no guilt. Allah is forgiving and merciful.

(2.172–73)

They denied the truth and uttered a monstrous falsehood against Mary. They declared: "We have put to death the Messiah Jesus the son of Mary, the apostle of Allah." They did not kill him, nor did they crucify him, but they thought they did.

Those that disagreed about him were in doubt concerning his death, for what they knew about it was sheer conjecture; they were not sure that they had slain him. Allah lifted him up to His presence; He is mighty and wise. There is none among the People

*of the Book but will believe in him before his death; and on the
Day of Resurrection he will be a witness against them.*

(4.156–59)

*Unbelievers are those that say: "Allah is the Messiah, the son
of Mary." For the Messiah himself said: "Children of Israel,
serve Allah, my Lord and your Lord." He that worships other
gods besides Allah shall be forbidden Paradise and shall be cast
into the fire of Hell. None shall help the evil-doers.*

*Unbelievers are those that say: "Allah is one of three." There is
but one God.*

(5.72–73)[49]

Muhammad and the Hijra

Perhaps the best place to begin with Muhammad is in the glories of Islamic civilization to which we have already referred.
When one looks at such achievements one might be rather more
easily tempted to think seriously about the man whose genius
stands at the back of such an amazing movement. However, to
suggest that Muhammad's importance stems in large part from
the movement that he originated, and to suggest that the movement is the result of his genius, betrays a very un-Islamic way of
viewing the man. For Muslims the importance of Muhammad
derives not from the Islamic movement or from his life or his
genius. Rather the movement and his life both derive their importance from the Quran and thence from God.[50]

Some scholars have made the point that if you compare Islam
with Christianity, the Quran parallels not the Bible but Jesus
Christ in Christian theology—that is, it is God's word to humankind. Muhammad then parallels not Jesus but Mary. His
greatness derives initially from the fact that he was the one who
was chosen to transmit God's message to humankind (see Nasr,
43). The traditional Islamic theory of inspiration gives no part to
the intellectual genius of Muhammad in the production of the
Quran. Muhammad, like Mary, was a passive instrument in the
hands of God. For this reason the prophet is pictured as unlettered: "the unlettered nature of the prophet demonstrates how
the human recipient is completely passive before the Divine. Were
this purity and virginity of the soul not to exist, the Divine Word
would become in a sense tainted with purely human knowledge

and not be presented to mankind in its pristine purity" (Nasr, 44). The prophet is thus unlettered for the same reason that Mary is a virgin: the Quran, like Jesus Christ, is purely the work of God.

Initially, then, for Muslims the significance of Muhammad derives from his function rather than from his person. His significance as a person is, however, quite important, for he is the interpreter par excellence of the Quran. His life and his sayings, as recorded in the Hadith, "traditions," are *the* great exegesis of the Quran. His interpretation of the Quran is primary and the most authoritative.

Having emphasized this Islamic view of the place of Muhammad, it is appropriate, however, that we return to the standpoint of Western scholarship to say that, although not necessarily denying the theological point of the divine origin of the Quran, we can assert that it *is* the work of Muhammad—because we can trace the origin of many of its ideas to the world in which Muhammad moved.

Like the Bible, the Quran contains elements clearly showing that it is historically conditioned:

And you shall recount in the Book the story of Mary: how she left her people and betook herself to a solitary place to the east.

We sent to her Our spirit in the semblance of a full-grown man. And when she saw him she said: "May the Merciful defend me from you! If you fear the Lord, leave me and go your way."

"I am the messenger of your Lord," he replied, "and have come to give you a holy son."

"How shall I bear a child," she answered, "when I am a virgin, untouched by man?"

"Such is the will of your Lord," he replied. "That is no difficult thing for Him. 'He shall be a sign to mankind,' says the Lord, 'and a blessing from Ourself. That is Our decree!' "

Thereupon she conceived, and retired to a far-off place. And when she felt the throes of childbirth she lay down by the trunk of a palm-tree, crying: "Oh, would that I had died and passed into oblivion!"

But a voice from below cried out to her: "Do not despair.

Your Lord has provided a brook that runs at your feet, and if you shake the trunk of this palm-tree it will drop fresh ripe dates in your lap. Therefore rejoice. Eat and drink, and should you meet any mortal say to him: 'I have vowed a fast to the Merciful and will not speak with any man to-day!' "

Then she took her child to her people, who said to her: "This is indeed a strange thing! Sister of Aaron, your father was never a wicked man, nor was your mother a harlot."

She made a sign to them, pointing to the child. But they replied: "How can we speak with a new-born infant?"

Whereupon he spoke and said: "I am the servant of Allah. He has given me the Gospel and ordained me as a prophet. His blessing is upon me wherever I go, and He has commanded me to be steadfast in prayer and to give alms to the poor as long as I shall live. He has exhorted me to honour my mother and has purged me of vanity and wickedness. I was blessed on the day I was born, and blessed I shall be on the day of my death; and may peace be upon me on the day when I shall be raised to life."

Such was Jesus, the son of Mary [Sura 19.16–34].

This is obviously an account of the birth of Jesus, though not that of the Christian Bible. Where did it come from? Those who know some of the medieval European versions of the birth of Jesus will see that it has something in common with them.[51] And the opinion of most scholars is that this account derived from traditions of Syriac Christianity. It is accepted tradition that Muhammad went with merchant caravans to Syria on at least two occasions.

Muhammad was born at Mecca in the Arabian peninsula somewhere about the year of 570 of Christian dating. His father Abdullah died before he was born, his mother Amina when he was six years old. He was thus cared for and brought to maturity by his grandfather Abd-al-Muttalib and his uncle Abu Talib. According to tradition, it was with the latter that he first went to Syria, when he was twelve years old. Later he was employed by a wealthy widow, Khadija, who sent him on another journey to Syria. On his return she proposed marriage and he accepted. Muhammad was twenty-five and Khadija was forty.

Muhammad appears to have lived a fairly prosperous and contented life for a period, but then to have gone through a time of dissatisfaction and a searching for a deeper truth. According to the traditions, when he was forty (that is, about 610 of the Christian era) he was called by God to be a prophet:

In the earliest of our authorities, Ibn Ishak (d. 768), the story of Mohammed's call reads: "In the year that Mohammed was called to be a prophet he went to Mt. Hira with his family in the month of Ramadan in order to devote himself to solitary religious exercises. 'One night,' the Prophet states, 'Gabriel came to me with a cloth as I slept and said: Recite! I answered: I cannot recite! So he choked me with the cloth until I believed that I should die. Then he released me and said: Recite (*Iqra*)!' The prophet hesitated, and twice again the angel repeated the harsh treatment. Then finally Mohammed asked: 'What shall I recite?' The angel said: 'Recite thou, in the name of the Lord who created—Who created man from clots of blood. Recite thou! For thy Lord is the most beneficent, who hath taught the use of the pen—hath taught man what he knoweth not' (Sura 96, 1–4). 'I awoke,' said Mohammed, 'from my sleep, and it was as if they had written a message in my heart. I went out of the cave, and while I was on the mountain, I heard a voice saying: O Mohammed, thou art Allah's Apostle, and I am Gabriel! I looked up and saw Gabriel in the form of a man with crossed legs at the horizon of heaven. I remained standing and observed him, and moved neither backwards nor forwards. And when I turned my gaze from him, I continued to see him on the horizon, no matter where I turned.' Finally the vision vanished, and Mohammed returned to his family" [Andrae, 43–44].

In order to understand what happened when Muhammad returned to Mecca reciting the verses that became the beginnings of the Quran (the "recitation"), we should look somewhat at the religious environment in which these events took place. The first important feature was a local Arabian cult centered in Mecca. The tribe in control of the cult were the Quraysh, a group very popular in the city and indeed in the whole of Arabia, for the cult center was visited by pilgrims from the entire Arabian peninsula. The central object in the cult was a black stone, a meteorite known as the Kaaba. It is probable that there was animal sacrifice; there was a rite of circumambulation of the black stone. The cult was centered on the worship of three female deities, the daughters of a high god, whose name, Allah, was an Arabic word *(Allah)* cognate with the Hebrew word for god, Elohim. Trees, wells, and springs were regarded as sacred, and there was a belief in thousands of spirit-creatures called *jinn* (thus the "genie" of Aladdin's lamp). In Mecca, in addition to the official cult, there was a guild of seers whose members received their esoteric knowledge from the *jinn*. The seer *(kahin)* gave forth his oracles in a style of rhymed prose, often obscure and cryptic. The *kahin* would regularly be asked for advice about important undertakings, lost articles, stray camels.

There was also a group who believed that there was only one God, Allah. They were the *hanif*s. According to Muhammad, Abraham, whom he regarded as the father of the Arabian people as well as of the Jewish people, was a *hanif*.

In the south of Arabia, Yemen, there was a strong Jewish population, and there were also Christians in the area—in Syria to the north, and in Yemen where they were of Coptic-Ethiopian strain.

Muhammad came to Mecca with his message. The Meccans apparently thought of him as a *kahin*. There is a tradition that for the first three years there were good relationships between Muhammad and the Quraysh, though there is another that the people rejected and mocked him. It is difficult to know whether the antagonism of the people generally and that of the Quraysh in particular developed about the same time or were occasioned by different parts of Muhammad's message. It is possible that the antagonism of the Quraysh developed later, only after they perceived in Muhammad a threat to their control of the Kaaba and the worship of the three goddesses, and thus to their place of privilege.

Muhammad's message was strictly monotheistic. He may have been influenced by the *hanif*s in this regard, or by Jews or Christians. His message was also highly eschatological, threatening a coming day of doom and judgment. The picture given in a number of the sections of the Quran is in composite form as follows.

When the blast shall sound, when the trumpet is blown and the sun is darkened and the stars thrown down, when mountains are shaken and the seas set boiling, when the heavens are split open and tombs are overthrown and earth is ground to powder—then the Lord will come with angels rank on rank and Gehenna will be brought out. (The overthrowing of the tombs and the trumpet blowing appear to reflect a primitive Christian view of the last days.) This will be a day of doom, a day of judgment. There will be a division: some faces will shine brightly, others will be scowling, dusty, in darkness. Some will be companions of the right hand; those on the left hand will be sent off to the fire. Then the scales will be brought out, and an atom's weight of good and an atom's weight of evil will be known. The good go to heaven and the evil to hell. Hell, Gehenna, is a place of flaming fire. Heaven is a glorious garden. (The beauty of heaven is described in some detail in Sura 78; there are many other details in Suras 55, 71, 76, 81, 82, 99, and elsewhere.)

And what is the basis of the division of those who are received into glorious paradise and those who are sent off to punishment in the flames? Those who are rewarded are those who fed the needy and beggars, who cared for orphans, who freed slaves, who were generous and God-fearing and pious.

Sent off to Gehenna are those who do not feed the needy, the stinters, those who devour their inheritance, who love wealth; those who pray without care; those who make big displays, but are not generous.

We moderns tend to regard such an obvious threat that the consequences of evil living are painful experiences in a horrific hell as a poor kind of motivation for doing good, but for Muhammad fear was clearly a central part of faith. "A believer should not only believe in the last day, but he should *fear* it—fear the judgment and the Lord of judgment . . . . 'Believers are they who tremble in fear before the Lord.' . . . Fear is the natural basic mood of piety; the pious man should be fearful" (Andrae, 60).

Another way of putting this might be to say that "religion is primarily a voluntary surrender in trust and faith" (Nasr, 27). To be a Muslim is to offer oneself in humble submission to God's divine will. In fact, the word *islam* means submission or surrender, and this idea is essentially an extension of the idea of fear—a healthy fear, a deep respect for the all-powerful God. A true Muslim is one who in fear surrenders to God and tries to live in God's way.

In the early Suras that portray a vivid picture of the last days there is some indication of what the life of a Muslim involves, but it is at a later stage, under new conditions, that a fuller picture is developed.

We have said that the people of Mecca rejected Muhammad's message. But there were a few converts. The antagonism of the Meccans, however, increased so much that Muhammad had to flee for a time to Ethiopia.

It was about eleven years after his call—that is, about 621 of the Christian era—that some pilgrims came to Mecca from Yathrib, a city some two hundred miles north of Mecca. While they were in Mecca they were apparently attracted by Muhammad's teaching and asked him to come and take over the leadership of their city. Muhammad accepted their invitation. In 622 he migrated to Yathrib, which became known as Medina, "the city." This migration is called Hijra, or Hegira, and it ushered in the year 1 in the Islamic reckoning of time.

But why should this event be so crucial that it determined the system of dating that Muslims use? If Christians dated their calendar from the birth of Jesus, why do Muslims date it not from the birth of Muhammad or from the call of Muhammad but from the Hijra? The crucial thing, I think, is that this was the turning point, the historical fulcrum of the Islamic movement. What was implicit became explicit, what was theory became practice, what had been heard and rejected was now accepted; failure was replaced by success. For Muslims this acceptance and practice and success are extremely important. Islam is no impractical ideal; it is an intensely practical system.

At Medina Muhammad organized the nascent Islamic community on the basis of the message he was continuing to receive from God. Then, using Medina as a base, he engaged in a series of military attacks against Mecca and after nine years of struggle, in 630, entered into Mecca victorious. The Quraysh offered no resistance. The images were thrown out of the Kaaba and it became a shrine to Allah, to God. Two years later Muhammad died.

This is the story in its barest outline. As in the case of the others of our breakthrough figures, the story was later greatly elaborated. Many of the details are directed toward indicating his universal significance. Thus, as for Gautama and for Jesus, remarkable events accompany his birth:

> When he was born, the palace of the Persian emperor trembled, fourteen of its towers fell, the Mazdaean sacred fire went out, a lake was dried up, a marvelous light shone from his mother's breast, this brightness spread as far as Syria, and the stars came so close that one witness was afraid they would fall on him. It was said of him that his body threw no shadow, that the flies would not settle on his garments, and that when his hair fell in the fire it did not burn.
>
> Also at the hour of Muhammad's birth angels rush to see the event. They brought a mattress and a coverlet so that his mother, though poor, might rest in comfort. A little later, while he was still an infant, the Prophet was visited by angels who bore a pitcher, a basin, and a towel to inaugurate the ritual ablutions that Muslims perform before offering prayers to God [Rodinson, 303].

Later, when he went on a journey with his uncle Abu Talib, a cloud shaded him from the sun as he rode along on his camel, and later a tree bent over him so that he was in its shade. A Christian monk, Bahira, recognizing the marks of his greatness, was able to find between his shoulders the seal of his prophethood. (Bahira seems to be a structural equivalent of Simeon and Asita.)

Like others we have studied, most notably Jesus and Krishna, Muhammad performed remarkable deeds. The woman who was his wet-nurse had an old female camel, and while the baby Muhammad was with her, the camel gave an abundance of milk; as did also her husband's flocks. Water was seen to spout from between the prophet's fingers. And on one occasion, he fed about eighty persons with a small amount of barley bread (Rodinson, 304–5).

Perhaps the most remarkable event was an experience like that of the shamans of northern Asia and North America, of journeying to heaven:

> One night angels appeared to Muhammad and prepared him for a night journey through Paradise. Gabriel, some of the legends say, awakened the Prophet, split his body from his neck to waist, and removed and washed his heart. As the angel returned Muhammad's heart to his body, he filled his soul with faith and wisdom. Purified, Muhammad mounted a fabulous creature named Buraq that had a woman's face, a mule's body, a peacock's tail—and the ability to cover in a single bound distance as far as the eye could see. Riding Buraq (who, tradition holds, had borne up other prophets before him) Muhammad passed through seven heavens and enjoyed the rarest privilege of all—seeing God's unveiled face. During the night journey, Muhammad met patriarchs, Old Testament prophets and angels in prayer in a celestial mosque. While in Paradise, Muhammad met Moses, whom he later described as "a ruddy-faced man." Jesus he depicted as freckled and of medium height; of Abraham he said, "Never have I seen a man more like myself" [Stewart, 24–25].

The essential function of this story seems to be close to that of the transfiguration in the case of Jesus: a mythic indication of his relationship to other prophetic figures.

In terms of the basic hero pattern, the account of Muhammad's life comes closest to that of Moses. For in both cases there are two major journeys. The first, utilizing the quest motif, shows the great encounter by God, the commissioning of the Prophet to his task. The second is a journey of the community—an escape from the alien environment, the establishment of the community on the basis of the message received.

There is a difference, however. In the case of Muhammad, the inimical powers are not overcome at the time of the escape, as they are for Moses. In the Jewish case, tyrannous Egypt is left behind and the Israelites set their faces toward the Promised Land into which God eventually brings them. In the Islamic case, the battle is at the end—and it is not a wiping out of evil powers but rather a taming of the opposition, an incorporation of Mecca into the Islamic system; even more, the bringing of Mecca into the very center of the system. For Jews, Egypt is overcome and left behind. The focus of their hope becomes, eventually, Jerusalem. For the Muslims, the Mecca left behind becomes their Jerusalem, their sacred city, the center of the Islamic world.

It was at Medina that details of Muslim life were worked out. We can see these details in many passages from the Quran; a number of them are included in the set of recitations from the Quran at the beginning of this section.

Instructions for Islamic life as set out in the Quran can be divided into two groups. The first group has to do with ritual or devotional acts; the second group with social obligation.

In the first group perhaps the most important injunction is the injunction to prayer. The full detail of what is involved in prayer for Muslims is not given in the Quran but the basis is set forth. According to tradition, God gave instructions for Muslims to pray five times a day—upon rising, at noon, in mid-afternoon, at sunset, and before retiring. Muslims pray facing toward Mecca; but there is an indication that early in his ministry Muhammad instructed his followers to pray facing toward Jerusalem and later changed it toward Mecca. When Muslims pray, their first words are indications of the greatness of God. A prayer that is almost invariably said is found at the beginning of the Quran, the first Sura, referred to as the Fatihah or "opening":

> In the name of God, the merciful, the compassionate
> Praise belongs to God, the Lord of all being,
> the all-merciful, the all-compassionate,
> the master of the day of doom.
> Thee only we serve; to thee alone we pray for succor.
> Guide us in the straight path,
> The path of those whom thou hast blessed,
> Not of those against whom thou art wrathful,
> Nor of those who are estranged [Arberry, 1].

Prayer, undertaken so frequently in this way, clearly orients the lives of Muslims toward God. Time is taken out from ordinary events with the result that those ordinary events are brought into the context of God and God's word. The discipline of prayer thus can be seen to be very effective in guiding a Muslim to *islam,* submission to God.

The second ritual action prescribed in the Quran is that of fasting. As is indicated there, the month when this occurs is the month of Ramadan, the time when Muhammad received the Quran from God (that is, the month when the initial revelation was given to Muhammad at Mt. Hira). The practice of fasting—Muslims neither eat nor drink from dawn to dusk during this month— functions very effectively to bind Muslims together in an awareness of their unity of common goals and serious intent.

Even more powerful psychologically for uniting Muslims is the great event of the pilgrimage. The commonly accepted interpretation of the injunction is that Muslims should visit Mecca at least once during their lifetime. What is provided here is the direct physical experience of the topography of Mecca and the surrounding area in a presentation of concrete symbols that introduce the lives of Muslims to the events of holy history, to the significant events of Muhammad's life that surround the central act of God's giving of the Quran. There is also provision for relating the Muslim to the lives of the first great Muslim, Abraham, and his son Ishmael. The effect of this is to give a quite concrete impression of the events of the faith and at the same time, with millions of others in attendance, an awareness of this great unified body of the faithful who five times a day all pray facing toward this center of the world, the city of Mecca. The pilgrimage to the city itself is thus a grand culmination of the thousands of times a Muslim has faced toward Mecca to pray.

The three injunctions mentioned so far comprise three of a set of basic practices referred to as "the five pillars of Islam." There is a fourth pillar of the same style as these—that is, it has to do with ritual action. This is the creed: "There is no god but God; and Muhammad is the prophet of God."[52] The creed is not presented anywhere in the Quran itself, but is a kind of summation of what the Quran is all about and of the conviction that God has spoken via Muhammad. I call this a ritual injunction because, although in strict terms Muslims are enjoined merely to speak these words and to meditate upon them carefully at least once in their lives, in normal practice a Muslim says them several times a day.

Each of these four ritual injunctions does two things. It focuses the lives of Muslims upon God, and it functions effectively to unify the people—which is what one would expect from a religious style that is so insistently monotheistic.

The fifth of the five pillars of Islam is almsgiving. This may effectively introduce us to the other kind of action that the Quran deals with, that of an ethical or social dimension. Although the giving of gifts is the only injunction on the social side that is included in the five pillars, the Quran has much to say about social responsibility. In Sura 2.177 there is reference to the way one should treat persons in various kinds of need. In the Quran there is a great deal of emphasis on the need for kindness and generosity and there are injunctions against killing and coveting.

There are also much more specific details, such as the section in Sura 2.178-79 relating to retaliation. This appears somewhat dependent on Jewish views of retaliation, and gets one into areas that border on the legal rather than the ethical. This system of retaliation was a more humane system than what obtained in Arabia before the time of Muhammad. It is an attempt to be strictly fair, to bar the use of an injustice received as a pretext for a massive battle against an enemy. The emphasis of the Quran itself, however, is that retaliation is a protection of life. Modern Western "humane" approaches tend to see capital punishment as a desecration of life. The argument here is that the act of retaliation is a way of emphasizing the preciousness of life.

A related area where there has often been criticism of the Islamic position is that of war. Christians have frequently argued the superiority of Christianity over Islam because it teaches peace, not war; turning the other cheek rather than retaliating. Some Christians have felt that the Quran by discussing war legitimates it, makes it too easily an accepted part of life, even hallows it. The counterargument of Muslims is that because Christians have banished war from normal consideration, insufficient guidelines have been given for determining when war is appropriate. The position of the Quran is clear: there are some circumstances in which war is necessary. The Quran offers no justification for aggression; fighting is legitimate if it is defensive—safeguarding the state against physical aggression; freeing Muslims from persecution, from being forced to worship idols (see Khan, 176–83).

Other areas that are dealt with in detail in the Quran include the treatment of women (see above, p. 113). The picture presented here suggests a fairly harsh treatment, a clear domination of women by men, and this has naturally been the cause of considerable criticism from those who accept contemporary emphases on the equality of men and women.[53] The practice of allowing men to have more than one wife has also received much criticism. It has been argued by Muslims, however, that the practice was probably introduced as a way of ensuring, in the rather militant society in which Muhammad lived, that all women were provided for, all able to be placed under the care of some male. Also, Muslims point out, it is emphasized that if one cannot be fair and impartial in one's dealings with a number of wives, one should have only one wife. Still, those who look to the equality of men and women regard Islamic polygamy as a system of inequality—one in which by the very structure of things women and men cannot meet each other on equal terms. But if one tries to think in positive terms about this, one can see it as an advance on other possible views. If one accepts that Muhammad is in this case culture-bound, to the extent that he cannot think in any other terms than that of males as dominant, one can also appreciate his focusing of this dominance into care and responsibility, over against the manipulation of women, the treating of them as sexual objects. (It is in this light also understandable that many Muslims find the clothing of Western women, which so often suggests sexual enticement and therefore corroborates the depiction of women as sexual objects, an extreme form of moral decadence.)

It has been mentioned in connection with Moses that a number of the injunctions of Torah have to do with legal aspects, and much of what is presented in the Quran and in the application of it in Islamic life also has this dimension. In addition, there are in Islam injunctions like those relating to ritual cleanliness among the Jews—such as the prohibition of wine, pork, carrion, and blood.

There are other themes of the Quran that are worthy of consideration. One is that of the relationship of Muhammad with Jews and Christians. The Quran mentions a large number of prophets including some on which a considerable amount is written— Abraham, Moses, Jonah, Joseph, David. All together there are some twenty-eight prophets mentioned, and among them is included Alexander the Great. Most of these prophets are from Jewish history, but they are not the classical prophets whose proclamations are recorded in the Hebrew Bible. Rather they are popular figures whose relationship to God is portrayed in some detail in Jewish materials.

In the Quran Jesus is also included as one of the prophets. Much of what Muslims believe is similar to that traditionally held by Christians: that he was born of a virgin, that he performed miracles, that he was the Messiah, the servant of God. However, there are two points where there are major disputes with Christians. According to the Quran Jesus was not crucified—he was taken up to heaven (Sura 4.156). Also he was not divine—for Muslims, to maintain that Jesus is divine is the epitome of the worst of errors, that of *shirk,* associating a creature with God. To associate a human being with God is a denial of the radical supremacy of God.

Muhammad himself is portrayed as the last or the seal of the prophets. His coming is supposed to have been foretold by Jesus. Tor Andrae thinks that this claim that Jesus foretold the coming of Muhammad was due to an error in which the promise of the Paraclete *(parakletos),* the "strengthener" (John 15:26), was misunderstood as a promise of the *periklytos,* the "illustrious one" (Andrae, 35). The claim that Muhammad was the last of the prophets, the end of the line, and the accompanying picture of Islam as the fulfillment of all that has gone on within Jewish and Christian history has been a considerable stumbling block in relations between Muslims on the one hand and Jews and Christians on the other. Christians quite naturally found it impossible to accept that what Jesus had done had now been superseded.

There is another point of dispute between Muslims and Christians. The Quran is strongly antagonistic toward the idea of the Trinity, that, as it puts it, "God is one of three." This is a variant on the problem of *shirk*, associating or confusing God and Jesus. But it takes us in another direction. The *Quran* is uncompromising about the fact that God is one. This is not just a matter of an assertion in the area of numbers. Muslims have argued that this conception of the unity of God has made them the most unified of all religious groups. Whether this claim is true is open to debate, for there clearly are in modern Islam, and there have been for many centuries within the Islamic community, quite deep tensions, strong rifts—for example, between the Sunni and Shi'a sects. It is true, however, that there is a kind of unification achieved around the view of the unity of God. Muslims have tended not to make distinctions, common in the Christian world, between spiritual and temporal, between religious and secular. Governing a country is as much a religious act as is preaching to worshipers in the mosque. In addition, there *is* justification for seeing Muslims as the least racially conscious of all peoples and the pilgrimage of Muslims from every part of the world to Mecca as a concrete demonstration of it.

The True Center

At this point it seems appropriate to return to noting similarities between the system presented by Muhammad and that of Moses. In both cases the interest is on religious action rather than on what one believes. Not that belief is unimportant; we have emphasized in the case of Muhammad that belief in the unity of God is an all-important element. Nevertheless, the focus of interest is on the life of the people, upon how a good Jew or a good Muslim should live. And parallel to the focus of Jews on *halakhah,* there is a Muslim emphasis on *shariah,* variously epitomized as "the highway of the good life" (Rahman, 117) and "the road that leads to God" (Nasr, 93).

Somewhat similar systems are also developed for determining what actions should be performed. Both develop ways of bringing the original texts to the different circumstances of later periods of history. Jews developed a distinction between written Torah and oral Torah, between what is found in the Bible and the traditions handed down from generation to generation on what great rabbis have said in relation to specific topics of the law. Two commonly accepted statements reveal two different aspects of the relationship between them as Jews see it. First, Jews have maintained that both oral and written Torah were given to Moses at Mount Sinai.

This is surely an attempt to maintain the full validity of oral Torah: for Jews, written Torah without the oral commentary is not Torah. But, lest one should think that Jews are historically naive in their tradition that both oral and written were given to Moses, there is a story about the visit of Moses to the academy of Rabbi Akiba, in the second century C.E. Moses was quite astounded and mystified by the kind of discussions he heard going on in the academy. He was somewhat gratified, though also further mystified, when at the end he heard Akiba say, "And this law was given to Moses at Sinai."

What was developed, then, was a system by means of which the ancient text could be applied in the context of a later, much different situation. One of the effects of this is the enormous importance that is given to learning in Jewish tradition—not theological learning, but practical learning: the hard debate of points of law becomes one of the supreme achievements of Jewish culture.

In the case of Muslims it is accepted that the central holy book, the Quran, is not exhaustive: for further specification of how Muslims should live there are needed additional materials. As indicated at the beginning of this section on Muhammad, the *hadith*, the "traditions" about the life of the prophet, are important because Muhammad's life is regarded as the prime exegesis of the Quran. Muslims learn how they should live partly by seeing the kind of life that Muhammad lived. But even then not everything is clear; and so, in a somewhat secondary role there are regularly accepted two other bases for authority in the Islamic system—*qiyas* (analogical reasoning) and *ijma* (consensus). The implication of these is that within the context of the community of the *ulama*, the spiritual leaders, and on the basis of analogy, the true path that Muslims should follow will be made plain.

The kind of pattern, then, that was set forth for the Jewish nation was extended by Muslims to cover a variety of nations. But within each of these Islamic nations the same basic principles applied, of a life established upon an ethical and ritual and legal system appropriate to those who have submitted themselves to God.[54]

The title of this chapter is "Burning Bush and Mountain Cave." As we reflect upon what we have seen in the cases of Moses and Muhammad, we naturally begin to wonder if this is not a misrepresentation. We have noted that in both cases there are two journeys—and the second journeys (exodus, Hijra) are far more important in reflecting the fact that for Jews and Muslims the community and its practical needs are central.

Still, I let the title stand as it is. The flame and the bush, the cave and the mountain, remain powerfully evocative symbols of the other side of the vision represented in Moses and Muhammad. If we understand that the community, not the individual, is central, we do well. These symbols point us to the true center—God.

V

ARMS FLUNG WIDE TO EMBRACE THE WORLD: JESUS

TEN HARD SAYINGS OF JESUS

Very early next morning he got up and went out. He went away to a lonely spot and remained there in prayer. But Simon and his companions searched him out, found him, and said, "They are all looking for you." He answered, "Let us move on to the country towns in the neighborhood; I have to proclaim my message there also; that is what I came out to do." So all through Galilee he went, preaching in the synagogues and casting out the devils.

(Mark 1:35–39)

"No one sews a patch of unshrunk cloth on to an old coat; if he does, the patch tears away from it, the new from the old, and leaves a bigger hole. No one puts new wine into old wine-skins; if he does, the wine will burst the skins, and then wine and skins are both lost. Fresh skins for new wine!"

(Mark 2:21–22)

Now they had forgotten to take bread with them; they had no more than one loaf in the boat. He began to warn them: "Beware," he said, "be on your guard against the leaven of the Pharisees and the leaven of Herod." They said among themselves, "It is because we have no bread.'' Knowing what was in their minds, he asked them, "Why do you talk about having no bread? Have you no inkling yet? Do you still not understand? Are your minds closed? You have eyes: can you not see? You have ears: can you not hear? Have you forgotten? When I broke the five loaves among five thousand, how many basketfuls of scraps did you pick up?'' "Twelve,'' they said. ''And how many when I broke the seven loaves among four thousand?'' They answered, "Seven.'' He said, "Do you still not understand?''

(Mark 8:14–21)

Jesus and his disciples set out for the villages of Caesarea Philippi. On the way he asked his disciples, "Who do men say I am?'' They answered, "Some say John the Baptist, others Elijah, others one of the prophets.'' "And you,'' he asked, "who do you say I am?'' Peter replied: "You are the Messiah.'' Then he gave them strict orders not to tell anyone about him; and he began to teach them that the Son of Man had to undergo great sufferings, and to be rejected by the elders, chief priests, and doctors of the law; to be put to death, and to rise again three days afterwards. He spoke about it plainly. At this Peter took him by the arm and began to rebuke him. But Jesus turned round and looking at his disciples, rebuked Peter. "Away with you, Satan,'' he said; "you think as men think, not as God thinks.''

(Mark 8:27–33)

Then he called the people to him, as well as his disciples, and said to them, "Anyone who wishes to be a follower of mine must leave self behind; he must take up his cross, and come with me. Whoever cares for his own safety is lost; but if a man will let himself be lost for my sake and for the Gospel, that man is safe. What does a man gain by winning the whole world at the cost of his true self? What can he give to buy that self back?''

(Mark 8:34–37)

So they came to Capernaum; and when he was indoors, he asked them, "What were you arguing about on the way?'' They were silent, because on the way they had been discussing who was the greatest. He sat down, called the Twelve, and said to them, "If anyone wants to be first, he must make himself last of all and servant of all." Then he took a child, set him in front of them, and put his arm round him. "Whoever receives one of these children in my name," he said, "receives me; and whoever receives me, receives not me but the One who sent me."

(Mark 9:33-37)

They brought children for him to touch. The disciples rebuked them, but when Jesus saw this he was indignant, and said to them, "Let the children come to me; do not try to stop them; for the kingdom of God belongs to such as these. I tell you, whoever does not accept the kingdom of God like a child will never enter it." And he put his arms round them, laid his hands upon them, and blessed them.

(Mark 10:13-16)

Jesus looked round at his disciples and said to them, "How hard it will be for the wealthy to enter the kingdom of God!" They were amazed that he should say this, but Jesus insisted, "Children, how hard it is to enter the kingdom of God! It is easier for a camel to pass through the eye of a needle than for a rich man to enter the kingdom of God." They were more astonished than ever, and said to one another, "Then who can be saved?" Jesus looked at them and said, "For men it is impossible, but not for God; everything is possible for God."

(Mark 10:23-27)

At this Peter spoke. "We here," he said, "have left everything to become your followers." Jesus said, "I tell you this: there is no one who has given up home, brothers or sisters, mother, father or children, or land, for my sake and for the Gospel, who will not receive in this age a hundred times as much—houses, brothers and sisters, mothers and children and land—and persecutions besides; and in the age to come eternal life. But many who are first will be last and the last first."

(Mark 10:28-31)

"You have learned that they were told, 'Eye for eye, tooth for tooth.' But what I tell you is this: Do not set yourself against the

*man who wrongs you. If someone slaps you on the right cheek,
turn and offer him your left. If a man wants to sue you for your
shirt, let him have your coat as well. If a man in authority makes
you go one mile, go with him two. Give when you are asked to
give; and do not turn your back on a man who wants to borrow.
You have learned that they were told, 'Love your neighbor, hate
your enemy.' But what I tell you is this: Love your enemies and
pray for your persecutors; only so can you be called the children
of your heavenly Father, who makes his sun rise on good and bad
alike, and sends the rain on the honest and the dishonest. If you
love only those who love you, what reward can you expect? Surely
the tax-gatherers do as much as that. And if you greet only your
brothers, what is there extraordinary about that? Even the
heathens do as much. There must be no limit to your goodness, as
your heavenly Father's goodness knows no bounds."*

(Matthew 5:38–48)

The Good News in the Synoptic Writings

The place to begin an approach to the study of Jesus has to be
the word used by early Christians when they put together the materials of the Jewish Bible and writings that had been accepted as
authentic Christian texts. The word used for the second set became in Latin *Novum Testamentum* and thence in English "New
Testament." But a better translation than "testament" is "covenant," the word we have seen used to describe the relationship
between God and the people of Israel.

The early Christians were convinced that a new relationship
had been instigated between God and humankind. Their proclamation of this new covenant was centered on the conviction that
Jesus was the Messiah, the anointed one of God—a figure long
thought of by Israel as the inaugurator of a new age.

Within the writings that comprise the witness to this conviction
about the new covenant there are three major corpuses (as well as
some minor writings). The first is the Pauline corpus, which com-
prises a series of letters written between A.D. 45 and 60 by Paul,
the first great missionary of the Christian church, to various of
the small Christian communities scattered throughout the eastern
half of the Mediterranean area. Some of these churches he had

established himself, others he had visited, others he had merely heard of. Sometimes he wrote in an effort to help where there were serious problems in the community; at other times he just wanted to give general encouragement. But in all cases what he attempted to do was to relate the life of Jesus to the specific or general needs of the people of the early Christian community.

The second important set of writings is usually referred to as the synoptic Gospels. These are the Gospels according to Matthew, Mark, and Luke. The word translated "gospel" is in Greek *euangelion,* cognate with another Greek word *angelos,* in English "angel." The key idea is message, news. An angel is a messenger (not somebody who floats around on wings); gospel is good news. The synoptic Gospels present the good news about Jesus as the Messiah by way of an account of his life and teaching. (The writing of Paul is no less "gospel," but the context is generally, as I have said, specific needs of early Christian churches.) These three are referred to as synoptics because they look at the life of Jesus from a similar perspective. Indeed, the correspondence between them is so close that scholars are in general convinced there has been borrowing of material from one to another. The general theory accepted today is that Mark was written first, and is perhaps the good news according to Peter, one of the first disciples of Jesus. It was probably written between A.D. 65 and 70. Matthew and Luke were written ten to fifteen years later, and probably used Mark as the basis of their accounts—for the events they share with Mark they follow his order and often his words— but also added materials from other sources. Again a large body of non-Markan material that these two present is so similar that many scholars think that they both drew on one or more common written sources, perhaps a collection of sayings of Jesus, now lost. An alternative view is that both were drawing upon an oral tradition of sayings of Jesus that had been transmitted in relatively similar form across the churches.

The term "synoptic" really points up the differences between these accounts of the life of Jesus and that of John—part of the third or Johannine corpus—which is of quite a different character. But it also is a presentation in the form of a life history of the good news about Jesus. The nature of the differences, and the implications of them, we shall explore later.

It must be emphasized that these Gospels are not primarily history. Paul refers to the events of Jesus' life only in passing, usually to illustrate or establish a point in his argument. The others deal more directly with the events of Jesus' life, but are clearly not interested in saying everything that could possibly be said. Their writings are a witness to the good news that they have heard and seen in the life and teachings of Jesus. Nevertheless, a life story does emerge, and again it is valuable to compare it with Campbell's "monomyth" and the other life stories we have seen.

In many respects (as already suggested) the story is like that of the Buddha. There is a call, an entry into the wilderness, a meeting with the tempter, which results in the defeat of the tempter (Satan); angels, messengers of God, strengthen Jesus and he returns to ordinary life and begins his ministry of teaching and healing.

Compared with the version of the Buddha's journey into the wilderness, what one notices are, first, that this occupies such a small part of Jesus' life story—a few verses each in Matthew and Luke, and forty days as against about seven years for the Buddha; and, secondly, that there is for Jesus no quest motif, only the battle motif. The call into the wilds is for Jesus the result of his already knowing in his baptism by John that he is anointed of God for a special task. The encounter with the alien powers is not a prelude to his finding the truth, but is directly related to how the vision he has is to be communicated to others.

As in the case of Moses and Muhammad, there is a second journey in the Jesus story. Certain features of the imagery of Paul and details of Luke and the early part of the Acts of the Apostles suggest that it functions in parallel to the exodus story.[55] The details briefly are as follows: Jesus, after a ministry chiefly in the area around the Sea of Galilee, sets off for Jerusalem. Here after his ride into the city of Jerusalem, the symbolism of which pointed to a clear proclamation of himself as the Messiah, he was accused of blasphemy and the forces of evil did their worst—he was tortured, and died an ignominious death by crucifixion. But death could not hold him, and he rose triumphant from death; and after forty days of showing himself to his followers he ascended from their sight. And then ten days later, on the day of Pentecost—the day on which Jews commemorate the giving, at Mount Sinai, of the Torah, the center of the Jewish covenant—

the Holy Spirit was poured out on all flesh, the new covenant was shown in its pan-human scope.

Let me explain that last statement. The Christian writers are not content merely to give a cosmic setting to the birth of Jesus, though they do this—in stories of angels and shepherds, and Magi (Zoroastrian priests from Iran who have an interest in a special astrological sign, the appearance of a distinctive star); and in the story of the miraculous birth—from a woman who was still a virgin (Matt. 1:18–2:14; Luke 1:26–2:20). But this cosmicizing is carried on at the end, too—and in very concrete terms. The kind of reconciliation that is seen being worked out in the life of Jesus in a quite localized setting is proclaimed in the story of the day of Pentecost as something for all the world in a reversal of the old Hebrew myth of the tower of Babel (see Thielicke, 287). The rifts among humankind, so powerfully symbolized in the myriad languages spoken, were bridged as Jesus' followers "began to talk in other languages as the Spirit gave them the power of utterance" (Acts 2:4).

But we are getting ahead of ourselves. What it is that is thus universalized at Pentecost must be clarified by looking at the details of Jesus' ministry of teaching and healing. First, the version of the synoptic Gospels.

The portrayal of the good news in the synoptics is a complex interweaving of three major strands: accounts of "signs"; various aphoristic sayings of Jesus, the most telling of which are best described, I think, as "hard sayings" or "radical sayings"; and stories Jesus told, usually referred to as "parables."

The signs are in the main healings—of persons with a fever; of the deaf, dumb, and blind; of lepers; of the "demon possessed" (the portrayals of these in the Gospels suggest such maladies as epilepsy and schizophrenia). There are a few other signs of a different order: Jesus feeds at one time five thousand persons, and on another occasion four thousand; he stills a storm; he walks on water. It should be noted that the word *semeion* used in the Gospels for these events means "sign" and not "miracle." That is, the central idea is not that they defy explanation. They are rather pointers to that of which Jesus speaks so often—the love of God, the reign of God.[56] The gospel narratives consist in a continual interplay between Jesus' embodying the love of God, communicating it to others in healing action, and his speaking it in "hard sayings" and parables.

The Gospel of Mark, which comes across as very direct, arresting, a little rough, has few parables, many "hard sayings." The first is intimately tied to our understanding of the nature of Jesus' signs. Very early in his ministry, we are told, Jesus was in Capernaum, a port on Lake Galilee, and one evening large numbers of the sick were brought to him and he healed them. The next morning his disciples found themselves surrounded by crowds looking for Jesus, but he was nowhere to be found. The disciples eventually did find him, out in a deserted spot in the countryside, and when they told him that there were people everywhere looking for him, he suggested that they move on (Mark 1:36). A surprising, even startling statement. The point seems clear—it is made in the temptation story in the other Gospels—Jesus is no popularity-monger. His wonderful acts are not done to "wow" the crowds, but to heal. He is no superman, no "Six-Million-Dollar Man." Indeed the only gospel story that appears to be a marvel unrelated to the human need of healing and nourishment is the story of his walking on the water (Mark 6:45–52).[57]

One of the most surprising aspects of Jesus' early teaching and healing is the antagonism that it draws from the seriously religious group, the Pharisees. Within the religious and political situation of the Jewish people at the time, the Pharisees were those who concentrated all their attention upon the requirements of Torah. Others wanted to throw off foreign (Roman) rule and initiate the Messianic age by violent political means—the Zealots, and there was at least one Zealot among the disciples of Jesus.[58] The Pharisees were convinced that the only way to make possible the coming of the Messiah was for the people to be faithful to God by fulfilling the injunctions of Torah. But when the Pharisees came face to face with Jesus they were horrified. Jesus invited a tax collector—a traitor indeed, for he was employed by the hated Romans to take money from his own people—to be one of his followers; he socialized with tax collectors and other "bad characters." And then on a solemn day when others were fasting, his disciples did not fast. And one Sabbath day his disciples plucked ears of corn from a field, a clear breaking of Sabbath injunctions against work (see Hertzberg, 115). Finally, Jesus healed a man who had a deformed arm, in the synagogue, on the Sabbath.

In Mark's account of these events (Mark 2:13-28) Jesus pictures the conflict between the Pharisees and himself as the result of a clash between new and old. You do not put a new patch on an old garment, he says; more tellingly, you do not put new wine into old wineskins: "fresh skins for new wine!" (Mark 2:22). The new vision requires new modes of expression; it must not be encased in old, set patterns. The new vision breaks through the old structures of purity and "goodness." Christians have seen in the life and teaching of Jesus a quality of perpetual newness—it can never be encased in any system. "New every morning is the love"[59] of God shown in Jesus, and it continually breaks through the restrictions that are so easily and so often placed upon it.

Other parts of the synoptic Gospels reveal further dimensions of this conflict between Jesus and the self-righteous. Jesus tells a parable—a term regularly used of stories that he tells using ordinary everyday situations, and which "project" the hearer beyond them into an understanding of the "reign of God," the term he uses to speak of the power of God's love, of which he is both witness and embodiment. It is the parable in which he contrasts two men praying. One, a Pharisee, thanks God that he is different from others, that he is not beset with the sinfulness that infects the lives of so many others. The other man, a tax collector, prays only for the mercy of God, acknowledging himself a sinner. Jesus' comment is that it is the second, not the first, who is in a right relationship with God.

Elsewhere Jesus talks of those who "blow trumpets" before they do good deeds so that everyone will know what they are doing. The point is clear: the great danger of "being good" is that your goodness becomes central, becomes your god. And we can see from the encounter between the Pharisees and Jesus in Mark 2 and 3 the problem with "goodness": the religious-minded fear to contaminate themselves, fear losing their purity, so they stay away from "bad characters," blind to the fact that they are persons who need love and healing. They fast, cut off from the joy that the disciples know of Jesus with them, the love of God around them. They are strictly disciplined in the keeping of the Sabbath—and cannot understand how this day can be a day of healing for those withered in limb and life.

The implications of this conflict are drawn in other areas also. A rich man comes wanting to be a disciple of Jesus, and Jesus tells him to go and sell everything he has and give all the money away. When the young man leaves, unable to take this step that would be so threatening to his perception of himself and to his security, Jesus is saddened and then makes another of those shock statements of his: "It is easier for a camel to go through the eye of a needle than for a rich man to enter the kingdom of God." Jesus' disciples respond with the expected response of folk wisdom: "Who then can be saved?" If not the good, then who? If not the rich, then who? Jesus takes them where they are and says that from a human point of view it is impossible, but with God all things are possible.

Peter then calls attention to the fact that he and the other disciples have left everything to follow Jesus. And Jesus assures him that what has been given up will be repaid a hundred times. But then he pronounces another hard saying: "But many who are first will be last and the last first."

As we read through the synoptic Gospels the light gradually dawns: the love of God in Jesus is something that breaks through all our established hierarchies, breaks down all our spurious securities. Jesus' disciples argue about which of them is the greatest; Jesus says, "If anyone wants to be first, he must make himself last of all and servant of all" (Mark 9:35). Parents bring children to Jesus and his disciples tell them to go away; but Jesus calls the children to him: "Whoever does not accept the kingdom of God like a child will never enter it" (Mark 10:15). Peter acknowledges Jesus as the Messiah, but then when Jesus explains that he must suffer and die, Peter says no! And Jesus says, first, "Away with you, Satan!" And then, to any who would follow him, he tells them to take up their cross! Lose themselves! "What does a man gain if he wins the whole world at the cost of his true self?" (Mark 8:36).

We may delve further into this portrayal of God's reign if we note the contrast that is made between two groups of persons: the "good," the Pharisees, whom we have already discussed; and those who have decided to follow Jesus, his disciples. The most telling portrayal is in Mark:

> Now they had forgotten to take bread with them; they had no more than one loaf in the boat. He began to warn them: "Beware," he said, "be on your guard against the leaven of the Pharisees and the leaven of Herod." They said among themselves, "It is because we have no bread." Knowing what was in their minds, he asked them, "Why do you talk about having no bread? Have you no inkling yet? Do you still not understand? Are your minds closed? You have eyes: can you not see? You have ears: can you not hear? Have you forgotten? When I broke the five loaves among five thousand, how many basketfuls of scraps did you pick up?" "Twelve," they said. "And how many when I broke the seven loaves among four thousand?" They answered, "Seven." He said, "Do you still not understand?" [8:14–21].

Here we have yet another hard saying: "Do you still not understand?" And when you read about twelve and seven basketfuls left over after the feedings of thousands of persons, you find yourself in sympathy with the disciples. What is the point of these numbers? Jesus talks about the leaven of the Pharisees, and the disciples do not realize that he is talking metaphorically, parabolically; they think he is referring to the fact that they have forgotten to bring bread! But then we see Jesus explaining one not very difficult parabolic statement by another that is much more obscure. What a strange method of teaching!

Somebody well versed in numerology might reason that the twelve refers to the twelve tribes of Israel, and seven is the perfect number for all the ancient world. So this must be saying that when Jesus feeds a multitude there is still enough left for the entire people of Israel, and for all the world. It must be an oblique reference by the early Christian community to the Eucharist, the bread and wine shared by all the members of the church. It seems to me, however, that that is a trifle too slick. The numbers may be important, but only secondarily. Primarily, they are intended as a stimulus to the disciples to think about what has been happening at these feedings. If they think it has been about filling stomachs, they have missed the point, just as they have missed the point of Jesus' talk about the leaven of the Pharisees. These marvelous deeds are signs, pointers to the meaning of accepting God's rule. And when they see this, they will begin to understand the meaning of his warning. For the difference between the Pharisees (and also the king, Herod, whom Jesus mentions in this section) and the disciples is not that the disciples are quicker at understanding what is happening: they are quite dull when it comes to seeing the fuller dimensions of the good news. (Indeed the hard sayings continue for the disciples; it takes a long time for them to understand what he is saying. It is only after he has been crucified, and beyond that, when they are convinced that he is not dead but alive, that they really begin to comprehend.)

There is, however, a great difference between the Pharisees and the disciples. The disciples may not *understand,* but they respond authentically to God's love lived out in a life of healing and nourishing; the Pharisees, as they are painted in the Gospels, are, as we have said, those who are so interested in "goodness" and "purity" that they can no longer respond to the liberating power of God's love. They keep asking Jesus for "signs" of God's kingly rule, blind to the numerous signs of God's love in action before their very eyes.

Whether this is true to the actual historical situation of the Pharisees and Jesus is a question that is impossible for us to answer. There is evidence from the history of Rabbinic Judaism, the Jewish inheritance from the Pharisaic party, that there was among many rabbis sensitivity of the kind that Jesus is portraying. But we miss the point if we look too closely at the Pharisees per se. They are incorporated in these Gospels as representatives of a danger that is always there for the good and the respectable of any age.

One further hard saying is important if we are to see the implications of what Jesus has been saying. This is Matthew 5:48. I have been using the *New English Bible* translation; the *Revised Standard Version* is somewhat more literal here: "Be therefore perfect, as your heavenly Father is perfect." The word translated "perfect" could be translated "complete" or "fulfilled." And this clearly is a help because to be perfect as God is, is humanly impossible. The implication of the verse is that we should fulfill our human destiny in the same way as God's nature is fulfilled. If human beings are created in the image of God (Gen. 1:27), it is in this sense: You are to be the children of your Father, who makes the sun rise and the rain fall on good and bad alike. God does not give good things to the good and hold them back from the evil. God's love does not discriminate. It is for all.

For those who have been captured by this vision, the implication is clear: one does not love neighbors and hate enemies; one loves one's enemies. "If somebody hits you on the right cheek, offer him the left also." "How many times should I forgive—seven times?" "No . . . seventy times seven" (Matt. 18:21–22). There is no end to the number of times you are to forgive.

All of this is predicated by Jesus on the nature of God. Jesus teaches his disciples to think of God as "our Father" (Matt. 5:45–48; 6:5–16), "your heavenly Father." Some indications of what that means are given in the parables. A son takes his inheritance and runs off and wastes it in debauched living. Later he is sorry and he returns home. His father welcomes him with open arms. The dead is alive again, the lost is found! That father is what God is like (Luke 15:11–32).

Some men are working in a vineyard. Some start early in the day, others several hours later, some only a few hours before the end of the workday. The owner of the vineyard had agreed upon a wage with the first group, but when the owner pays all the workers the same, those in the first group complain bitterly. The owner makes the point that he has been fair to them. If he has been generous with the others who came later, they have no reason to complain (Matt. 20:1–16). The point is clear: God's generosity is unbounded. If we begrudge it, we miss the whole point of God's love.

One may still find this highly impractical as a basis for living. Surely, someone will say, you cannot be indiscriminate as God is with sun and rain. Surely you have responsibilities with your family first; later, when all those responsibilities have been fulfilled, you might think about helping somebody else. And surely we cannot take seriously the suggestion that if somebody takes your shirt, you should offer him your coat as well! But this statement of Jesus reminds me of a Zen story:

Ryokan, a Zen master, lived the simplest kind of life in a little hut at the foot of a mountain. One evening a thief visited the hut only to discover there was nothing in it to steal.

Ryokan returned and caught him. "You may have come a long way to visit me," he told the prowler, "and you should not return empty-handed. Please take my clothes as a gift." The thief was bewildered. He took the clothes and slunk away. Ryokan sat naked, watching the moon. "Poor fellow," he mused, "I wish I could give him this beautiful moon" [Reps, 12].[60]

The Zen monk knows the importance of what Jesus is saying: travel light. He knows that abundance of life is not to be found in things possessed. In the Zen case, a breaking through our self-centered clinging to the things of this world is achieved by a kind of intellectual game. There is the well-known example, the *koan:* "The mountain is a mountain. The mountain is not a mountain. Ah! There is the mountain again."[61] This typical problem for a Zen student to meditate on is aimed at breaking through one's preconceptions about the nature of the universe, about the nature of any particular phenomenon. The person who lives with typical clinging to the things of the world is a person who lives at the level of the first statement, a direct acceptance of mountains as mountains, of things as things. The second stage to which this *koan,* "problem," projects you is the stage in which you realize the relativity of everything, realize that each specific phenomenon is but a reflection of a unity beyond. Each specific element of the environment is thus devalued, being seen as *mere* phenomenon, not fully real; reality is elsewhere. The stage beyond that is one in which you can bring these two together, accept the mountain for what it is, knowing full well its relativity, its relatedness, but knowing that it has its part to play within the context of life lived in this particular dimension.

In the Zen tradition a person is taken through a radical breaking down of intellectual preconceptions, into a more realistic acceptance of the things of the world as they are, to a point where one can take or leave what is there, where one can enjoy what is given. If one has arrived at the point of saying, "Ah! The mountain is there again," one can really enjoy the mountain. Like Ryokan, one can really enjoy the moon!

Jesus, it seems to me, does the same kind of thing in his hard sayings as Zen *koan*s aim to do. His aim is to project us beyond our self-centered clinging, beyond the commonly accepted way of living, which is ultimately, he knows, so unfulfilling. His hard sayings are an attempt to throw us into another dimension, to propel us to a point where we are able to live from a different perspective. The basis of his position, however, is not a merely intellectual thrust. His method is not just to startle one intellectually—even at a very deep level (the *koan*s are very deep). Jesus' startling goes on thoroughly within the context of the nature of God: his hard sayings are an impetus to realizing the love of God. And in the extreme form that he gives in the Sermon on the Mount, what he portrays is the love of God as indiscriminate, unbounded generosity. And beyond that portrayal he is saying, "Be like God in this way: this is the way to live." The emphasis of Jesus' words and actions is that one lives authentically by living one's life in the context of the generosity of God.

If one looks again at the life of Jesus in this light, one can see that the form that the hero story takes is thoroughly in keeping with the vision that he presents. What happens in the birth stories, his being born in the remote town of Bethlehem, in a stable among cows and donkeys, down there with the animals, laid in a manger, lying on straw—all this is a profound demonstration of the generosity of God. His life is portrayed as that of one who would embrace the whole world with this generosity. In his first major encounter with evil powers in the temptation story, it is the question of how one brings human beings to realize and respond to God's love with which he wrestles. In the later encounter with evil, in his death on the cross, one sees in a moment what his whole life is about, the total self-giving love of this one with his "arms flung wide to embrace the world." So deep is the love and generosity of God that he who brings it to us in a human life is prepared to go even to death to enable it to be realized in human experience.

But does it mean, then, that one has to die as Jesus did on the cross, that one has to be a martyr, if one is to follow the way that he sets forth? If that is *the* way, is it not terribly impractical? How are we to understand these radical statements about how one should live?

Scholars have debated a great deal about how Jesus intended his words to be taken. One idea is that they are intended as impossible ideals that provide a continual dynamic, an impetus to strive always for something better. Another is that Jesus was speaking in the context of an apocalyptic vision, an unveiling of the end, a revelation of the world as it will be seen when all is brought to its consummation; and, more specifically, that Jesus saw himself as instigating the final days and was therefore prepared to demand something quite impractical.

Whatever the actual situation of Jesus' life and his ideas, Christians down through the centuries, attempting to take his words seriously, have come to the realization that a difficult decision has to be made. One might try to be a Mother Theresa—that would seem at first glance to be the kind of life that Jesus is calling us to live. But if all Christians followed such a path, there would soon be no Christian community, for there would be no Christian families. Many other Christians, therefore, have decided that their relationship to this vision has to be worked out in the context of family life and of the ordinary world. It is not easy to decide what one should do if one is to take Jesus seriously at that level; but it is clear that if one takes Jesus seriously, the life of a family will be different from what it is if one looks out only for oneself, or if a family thinks only of itself. The focus of the life of Jesus is service: the family that lives in the context of the generosity of God will be a group of persons attempting to be mutually generous and attempting to carry this generosity out into the world, "embracing the world with the love of God."

We have said that the crucifixion of Jesus epitomizes the life that he lived: he lived and died with his arms flung wide to embrace the world with the love of God. It is in this context that one may also delve further to understand the significance of the resurrection, Jesus' rising from death.[62]

What exactly happened? This question is inherently interesting because to say that somebody rose from death is so astounding a claim. Certain details are significant, it seems to me, for indicating what the resurrection is *not*. Many Christians argue for *full bodily* resurrection of Jesus; yet the fact that, in a number of cases, the persons to whom Jesus appeared—for example, Mary, who saw him in the garden, and the disciples walking on the road to Emmaus—did not recognize him, suggests that there was something different about the form in which he appeared to them—different from his form before his crucifixion. And Paul (whose discussions of the resurrection are the earliest in the New Testament) counted himself one of those to whom Jesus had showed himself after his resurrection, yet Paul's own experience was of a blinding light as he was traveling along the road to Damascus where he was going to persecute the Christians in the small Christian community just beginning to develop there. Paul apparently saw his own experience as of the same order as that of those to whom Jesus is reported in the synoptic Gospels to have shown himself between his resurrection and ascension. This suggests that the idea of a physical body does not fit his understanding of the resurrection, and indeed in discussing the resurrection he refers to "a spiritual body" or a "glorified body" (1 Cor. 15:35–49).

There have been many attempts down the centuries to explain, or explain away, the story of the resurrection—for example, that Jesus was taken down from the cross but was not really dead and so revived while he was in the tomb; or that he was not even crucified, that somebody else was crucified in his place. The most recent attempt to explain the stories has been via parapsychology—the idea being that the conditions of the time were exactly those in which one expects persons to have visions of the kind that are reported in the Gospels. The combination of the extraordinary and violent death and the intense emotional involvement of his disciples with him could easily give rise to such visions.

It seems to me, however, that we have no way of knowing what precisely happened, no *basis* for such explanatory theories. All that we know is that the gospel writers report that the tomb was empty, and that there was a profound change in the lives of the disciples: they took on new life, they were a new people. The link between these two can perhaps best be seen in theological terms—in the conviction that this one who lived a life so profoundly in touch with God had himself transcended death; death had no power over him. It has been suggested that the story of the empty tomb is the *response* of faith, not the *basis* of faith[63]—and this is in keeping with what I am arguing. Thus, theologically speaking, the resurrection is not a reversal of the death on the cross but a realization of what is inherent in it. Faith in the risen Lord involves the conviction that he who lives with arms flung wide to embrace the world with the love of God is not one whom death can finish.

Also problematic—particularly in the context of this comparative treatment of religious breakthrough figures—is the claim that Jesus is divine. In the synoptic Gospels, apart from one or two instances, what seems to be the picture is that of Jesus as a man, the Messiah, the anointed one of God.[64] As we have suggested, the stories relating to the birth of Jesus are best understood as an attempt to express the conviction that the life of Jesus is of cosmic significance. But the claim that he is God in human form is nowhere given direct expression.

On this score, the two other major corpuses—the Pauline letters and the Gospel of John—are quite different.

Jesus in the Pauline Letters

The development that can be traced in these different portrayals of who Jesus is helps in understanding what is claimed about the other figures we have studied. Virtually never has there been an attempt on the part of Jews to claim Moses as divine, or of Muslims to claim that Muhammad was divine. There is good reason for this. For both Jews and Muslims, to suggest that a human being can be in any sense identified with God is a gross error. The view of God that is presented in these traditions emphasizes radically the distinction between God and the world, between God and humankind. God is far beyond our imaginings, certainly not one to be portrayed in the form of images, or to be thought of as coming into human form.

Christians have been less stringent in their portrayal of the greatness of God. In this respect they have come closer to the picture that one sees with Buddhists and Hindus in referring to their great religious leaders. The Buddhists developed, some hundreds of years after the death of the Buddha, a doctrine known by the term *trikaya,* "the three bodies." According to this portrayal, the Buddha has three bodies—*dharmakaya,* the body of *dharma* (teaching, law); *sambhogakaya* (the body of bliss); and *nirmana-kaya* (the body of transformation or manifestation). The last mentioned of these is the body in which Buddha was seen in human form in India in the sixth century B.C. *Sambhogakaya* is a form in which the Buddha is seen by the saints, perhaps parallel to the form of Jesus in his transfiguration or his resurrection appearances. This is the appearance of the Buddha as he unveils himself to the eyes of faith. But beyond these manifest forms there is the "body of *dharma,*" which is usually equated in Buddhist thought with other words such as *shunyata,* "nothingness, emptiness," or *tathata,* "suchness." These terms are used to refer to the essential ontological basis of all that is. The implication of the doctrine of *trikaya* is that what one sees in human form in the life of the Buddha is none other than a manifestation of the central reality of the universe (see Smart, *Religions,* 82–89).

As we have seen in our discussion of Krishna, a similar portrayal is presented there. Krishna is seen as a manifestation on to the stage of mundane history of the being who is the central reality of the universe, the Supreme Person, God. To see Jesus in the context of the thinking about Krishna and the Buddha is not to deny that there are fine differences, in the way these figures are portrayed, in terms of the relationship in them of human to divine. Often when Christians have talked about Buddhist and Hindu doctrines they have seen them as examples of a Christian "heresy" about Jesus—the Docetic heresy, a view that Jesus only *appeared* to be human, was not fully human. And certainly Christians have been much more emphatic that Jesus is both *fully* human and *fully* divine. But within the various corpuses of the New Testament writings there are differing emphases in relation to this—and, as I have said, one can see in Paul and John quite different views from those found in the synoptic Gospels.

Perhaps the best way of bringing into focus the disparate positions that are developed is to note initially the words of Peter on the day of Pentecost as they are reported by Luke in the Acts of the Apostles:

Men of Israel, listen to me. I speak of Jesus of Nazareth, a man singled out by God and made known to you through miracles, portents, and signs, which God worked among you through him, as you well know. When he had been given up to you, by the deliberate will and the plan of God you used heathen men to crucify and kill him. But God raised him to life again, setting him free from the pangs of death, because it could not be that death should keep him in its grip. . . . The Jesus we speak of has been raised by God, as we can all bear witness. Exalted thus with God's right hand, he received the Holy Spirit from the Father, as was promised, and all that you now see and hear flows from him. . . . Let all Israel then accept as certain that God has made of this man, whom you crucified, both Lord and Messiah [2:22–24, 32–33, 36].

In this portrayal, Jesus is a man whom God takes and makes Messiah and Lord. But this is a far cry from the portrayals that one finds in Paul and John. Why such a change? In order both to see the change and to answer the question, it is imperative that we look in some detail at what these writers say and the background against which they say it.

The most important situation in the development of Paul's understanding of what Jesus' life meant had to do with the relationship between Jews and non-Jews in the young Christian community. The initial question was whether a gentile had to become a Jew in order to be a follower of Jesus the Messiah. There were other variants on this theme: Is it appropriate, for example, for a Jewish Christian to eat, to sit at table, with a non-Jewish Christian—given the fact that, for Jews, gentiles were seen as essentially unclean, polluting? The picture from both Acts and from Paul's letter to the Galatians suggests that there was considerable dispute among the early Christians on these issues. One camp, the "Judaizers" (Acts 11:2), maintained that non-Jews must first become Jews, must be circumcized before they are allowed to enter the Christian community. Peter seems to have vacillated somewhat, being convinced by a dream that distinctions between Jews and gentiles, between clean and unclean, were untenable (Acts 10:9–48); but then, under pressure from others, apparently also refraining from having meals with gentile Christians (Gal. 2:11–14).

The beginnings of his strong picture of what Jesus had done were worked out by Paul in his letter to the Galatians against the background of his anger at Peter's vacillation. What he states quite clearly is that it is not necessary for non-Jews to be circumcized before they become Christians. But he says this in the context of a bold statement about the significance of Jesus for human life. His picture goes something like this: human beings have been created for a close relationship with God. This relationship has been broken, marred by human sinfulness. The result is a continuing quest (evident in the many religious sects of the Roman world) for salvation. In terms of Jewish understanding, Paul sees this as a quest for righteousness, for *justification,* a right relationship with God.

The Jews of the Pharisaic tradition, which Paul knew well because he had been a Pharisee, saw the fulfilling of Torah as the way in which a person could be right with God. But Paul argues, somewhat from his own experience, that on these grounds no one can be justified. One may fulfill the law in every detail but then realize more than ever that one is not right with God. Paul takes up a theme that one can find in Jesus' words to and about the Pharisees—that those who are good, very good, may by virtue of their goodness become archetypes of human sinfulness, a marred relationship with God.

Paul comes to the realization that nothing that humans can do can restore the relationship between God and humankind. It is by the grace of God alone that we are saved. *God* restores the broken relationship as we are identified with the one who, although righteous, died. Because he died (in our place, as it were) we are made righteous in him. Our part is merely to accept God's grace, in faith (Gal. 2:16). As we accept the grace of God in faith, we are granted new life, a life *in* Christ, by the power of the Holy Spirit. We become those who *live* because Christ lives in us (Gal. 2:20).

Central to this vision for Paul is the freedom that it brings to Jew and gentile alike. Life under Torah is like the life of a slave; life under grace is that of a son (Gal. 3:26; 4:1-11). In the law, in the fulfilling of Torah, there is a binding quality because a person's life becomes so centered upon the fulfilling of the law that the worship of God, a right relationship with God, becomes impossible. Not that Paul saw Torah as evil. On this score he made two essential points: first, that Abraham was saved by his faith and not by his adherence to Torah; secondly, that Torah was a kind of tutor, or as someone has suggested, a "baby-sitter"[65] keeping watch over the people until the coming of Christ—that is, one might see Torah as a setting of the stage, the backdrop against which the significance of the life of Jesus could be understood and appropriated.

Thus, in the life of Jesus something new has taken place. In him, by the grace of God, a new relationship between God and human life has been established. There are new possibilities in living, a new freedom. Not that this freedom is license, for that also is really slavery; Paul draws out the strong ethical obligations involved in being free—Christians are free, in love, to serve each other as slaves (Gal. 5:13). Paul distinguishes between those who live their lives in the context of what God has done, those who live "in the Spirit," and others who live in the context of their "lower nature" (the Greek word *sarx,* "flesh," is thus translated in the *New English Bible*). The harvest of the Spirit, he says, is love, joy, peace, patience, kindness, goodness, fidelity, gentleness, self-control (Gal. 5:22).

Continually throughout his writings Paul establishes what God has done in Christ, and then goes on to exhort Christians to live in the context of what God has done. But he is emphatic above all else that it is not what Christians do that save them, not their good deeds or lack of them that restores the broken relationship between God and humanity—this is the act of God alone in Jesus Christ.

Paul draws on many images to portray what God has done in the life of Jesus. He utilizes the Jewish sacrificial system as a basis for understanding what has taken place, seeing Jesus' death on the cross as in some sense parallel to the death of sacrificial animals in which God and the sacrificer are brought together in a relationship of communion.[66] But he develops this theme of the restoration of the relationship using other images: seeing Christ as the "redeemer," seeing God as making peace with the world in Jesus Christ. And the portrayal of the breaking down of barriers is carried forth in Paul's understanding of what is done in the world: in Christ the walls of distinction that have ruled in human thought and action—such as those between Jew and Greek and between male and female—are smashed, broken down. In this new vision of humanity, all are one in Christ (see Barth, 39–51).

Gradually it becomes clear that if God is acting in this manner in the life of Jesus, restoring human life through the death of Jesus, then Jesus must be seen to have some very special relationship with God. Inevitably, Paul must attempt to say more precisely who Jesus is. And perhaps the fullest statement is that found in one of the later letters, in Philippians:

> For the divine nature was his from the first; yet he did not think to snatch at equality with God, but made himself nothing, assuming the nature of a slave. Bearing the human likeness, revealed in human shape, he humbled himself, and in obedience accepted even death—death on a cross. Therefore God raised him to the heights and bestowed on him the name above all names, that at the name of Jesus every knee should bow—in heaven, on earth, and in the depths—and every tongue confess, "Jesus Christ is Lord," to the glory of God the Father [2:6–11].

In this there is the assertion both of Jesus' original and essential divine nature and of his thorough entry into the human condition, of his self-emptying, "making himself nothing." An even higher vision of who Jesus is appears in Colossians:

> [God] rescued us from the domain of darkness and brought us away into the kingdom of his dear Son, in whom our release is secured and our sins forgiven. He is the image of the invisible God; his is the primacy over all created things. In him everything in heaven and on earth was created, not only things visible but also the invisible orders of thrones, sovereignties, authorities, and powers: the whole universe has been created through him and for him. And he exists before everything, and all things are held together in him. He is, moreover, the head of the body, the church. He is its origin, the first to return from the dead, to be in all things alone supreme. For in him the complete being of God, by God's own choice, came to dwell. Through him God chose to reconcile the whole universe to himself, making peace

through the shedding of his blood upon the cross—to recon-
cile all things, whether on earth or in heaven, through him
alone [1:13–20].

Here there is a marvelous portrayal of the relationship of Jesus to
God, to the world, to the church. Jesus is seen as the image, the
form visible within the world, of God who is invisible: looking at
him one is able to see the essential nature of God. But also Jesus is
portrayed as the one in whom everything, the entire universe, is
created and sustained. He is also the origin and head of the
church, which is portrayed as his body. But then Paul sees that the
universe, cut off from God, is in Jesus restored, reconciled,
brought to a new relationship of peace.

Jesus in the Johannine Gospel

The writer of the Gospel "according to John" accepts the
Pauline view of Jesus, and incorporates it into his narrative account of Jesus' life.[67] Scholars have long noticed the vastly different atmosphere of the life of Jesus in the synoptic Gospels
from that portrayed in the Gospel according to John. As well as
there being many differences of detail there is also a quite different vocabulary, such that it seems virtually impossible that
Jesus could have spoken both in the manner that one finds in the
synoptics and in the manner that one finds in John.[68] The generally accepted picture among critical scholars today is that, more
than the other gospel writers, the writer of John incorporated into
the sayings of Jesus his own meditations upon the significance of
Jesus' life. And he does it in a manner that reveals his vision of the
stupendous significance of the life of Jesus for the world.

It is clear from the opening of John, where the mythic portrayals of the synoptics are replaced by a highly sophisticated concep-
tual statement about who Jesus is, that this writer wants to
present him, in no uncertain terms, as God coming onto the stage
of the world, entering into human life, into human history. Utilizing a Greek concept of *logos,* "word," John portrays Jesus as the
self-expression of God. The same self-expression that was evident
in the creation of the world has now come in human form, in

human flesh, and "pitched his tent among us." The subsequent picture that is presented is a complex interweaving of certain key themes that present the significance of Jesus for human life.

Two motifs I regard as central. The first is the set of statements introduced by the phrase "I am." Jesus indicates that he is the bread of life (6:35), the light of the world (8:12), the door of the sheepfold (10:7), the good shepherd (10:11), the vine (15:1, 5); and "before Abraham was, I am" (8:58). As well as incorporating the clear implication that Jesus is God, the one who is able above all to say (following Exod. 2:14) "I am," there is here a powerful use of symbols from everyday experience, symbols that had a rich history in both Jewish and non-Jewish religious movements of the area in which the Christian message was being spread. Many of these statements about who Jesus is are linked with accounts of miracles or signs that Jesus performed. The signs thus become signs in a new sense in this Gospel: not manifestations or expressions of the reign of God, but rather pointers to the way in which Jesus affects human life. Jesus thus can be seen as one who feeds five thousand, and therefore as the one who gives bread, the essential sustenance for human life; as one who heals a man blind from birth, and thus as bringing light into the darkness of human life; as raising Lazarus from death, and thus as the one who gives life, restores life, to all who turn to him. The specific physical transformations that take place under his hands are seen as pointers to a wider activity, an even more profound effect in the lives of his followers.

The other important motif in this writer's understanding of the life of Jesus is the word *doxa,* "glory." A key point is that the first of Jesus' miracles or signs, which he performs at Cana in Galilee, is summed up as a manifesting, a showing forth of his glory (John 2:11).

If one turns to this first sign in John after looking at the synoptic portrayal of Jesus' signs, one cannot help feeling a little disappointed, even embarrassed. For here there is no picture of the tender, touching Christ; moreover, there is here no crying human need. There is a wedding reception, a typical Jewish wedding: the guests drink too much and they run out of wine. Jesus' mother prods him to do something about it; he rejects her entreaties, but eventually capitulates and water is transformed into wine! In

John's version of the life of Jesus, the first miracle is disappointing in its seeming triviality, its frivolity.

Another detail of this story renders it even more problematic. There are six stone water pots standing by and Jesus commands that these be filled to the brim with water, and it is this that becomes wine. Each of these jars holds twenty to thirty gallons of water. A hundred and fifty gallons of wine for one party is sheer irresponsible extravagance!

But if these jars are a problem, they also begin to provide a clue for interpreting the events. For the jars, we are told, are for the Jewish rites of purification. Scholars have observed that the writer of John in these early chapters contemplates at some length the relationship between the old covenant and the new. In a style that is reminiscent of, and perhaps draws on, the picture in Mark 3:11, that the new wine of the gospel requires fresh skins, not hard, old skins, here in the changing of water into wine John seems to be suggesting the transformation of the old into the new.

But the most important theme for understanding the sign is the statement about "glory." The term "glory" is found before the account of this first miracle, in John 1:14: "We have beheld his glory, the glory as of the only son from the Father, full of grace and truth." This suggests that there is a particular quality to the divine presence in, to God's self-disclosure to, human experience. And this squares with earlier uses, for in the Septuagint, the Greek version of the Jewish Bible, the word *doxa* translates the Hebrew word *kavod,* which means literally "weight, heaviness." In the Hebrew Bible *kavod* refers especially to the manifest presence of God—at Mount Sinai and Mount Horeb, in the tabernacle and in the temple. The image of "heaviness" suggests how overwhelmingly awesome is God's self-revelation to human life. The associated imagery is frequently visual—God is manifested to human experience in a brilliance like flames, in a shimmer of light.

Other verses in John where the word is used throw light on how this writer understands the marvel of the presence of God. The word occurs only rarely until the story of the raising of Lazarus, with its assertion that Jesus is life. From this time Jesus continually points forward to his death. He indicates that the time has come, as he says (12:23), "for the Son of Man to be glorified."

And then, "In truth, in very truth I tell you, a grain of wheat remains a solitary grain unless it falls into the ground; but if it dies it bears a rich harvest" (12:24). Gradually one realizes that although the glory of Christ may be seen in the changing of water into wine, and in his other miracles, the full glory is seen in his crucifixion, in his being lifted up from the earth (12:32), in this death that becomes the basis of a rich harvest in the gathering together of the scattered children of God (11:52), in Jesus' drawing all persons to himself (12:32).

There is another, later verse that is helpful: "The glory which thou gavest me I have given to them that they may be one as we are one; I in them and thou in me, may they be perfectly one" (17:22). In this verse Jesus is referring to those who will come to faith through the apostles—that is, the members of the Christian community—and he prays for their unity.

In one of the tales of the Hasidim collected by Martin Buber, there is a story from the life of the Baal Shem Tov, the eighteenth-century founder of that vibrant Jewish movement:

> At the festival of Simhat Torah, the day of rejoicing in the law, the Baal Shem's disciples made merry in his house. They danced and drank and had more and more wine brought up from the cellar. After some hours, the Baal Shem's wife went to his room and said: "If they don't stop drinking, we soon won't have any wine left for the rites of the sabbath, for Kiddush and Havdalah." He laughed and replied: "You are right. So go and tell them to stop."
>
> When she opened the door to the big room, this is what she saw: The disciples were dancing around in a circle, and around the dancing circle twined a blazing ring of blue fire. Then she herself took a jug in her right hand and a jug in her left and—motioning the servants away—went into the cellar. Soon after she returned with the vessels full to the brim [Buber, 52–53].

In the Gospel of John there is no theory of the atonement such as one finds in Paul, no working out on the basis of the sacrificial system or in psychological terms what it is that takes place when Jesus dies on the cross. Rather, we are presented with a kind of impressionistic witness to what happens when persons stand before the cross. It is here that the glory of God is seen in its fullness, and in the rich harvest that comes from Jesus' death, where human beings are one in him who is one with God, where his followers embrace each other in a circle of flame.

One can see, then, that the first unveiling of the shimmer of God's presence in human form, the first sign at Cana, and the last great manifestation of it interpret each other. The joy and exuberance of the transformation of water into wine find their fulfillment in the cross where there is seen that profound transformation of human life best portrayed in the transformation of water—tasteless, colorless, odorless—into fine wine, with its vibrant flavor, its rich sparkle, its delicate aroma.

We have said that in the story of Jesus there are, as with Moses and Muhammad, two journeys. But now it becomes clear that there are two stories!

In that of the synoptics there are two journeys, two forays against the powers of evil, one out into the wilderness, the other down into the domain of anguish and suffering and death—and from both Jesus emerges victorious. In John's version, however, there is no account of the temptation in the wilderness, only the journey into death. But even this is different. No story of the agony in the garden to set the scene of descent into death. And no descent, but rather an elevation, a lifting up ("as the serpent was lifted up by Moses in the wilderness"—John 3.14) granting to all a *darshana*, a vision of the glory of God.[69]

VI

BREAKTHROUGH TO THE GLOBAL VILLAGE

A Theology/*Darshana* of Breakthrough

Behind everything written thus far is the crucial question of how we at this particular point in history should relate ourselves to these great religious figures. Traditionally any given community that has identified itself in relation to one of these figures has been directed by the vision presented in the life and teaching of that particular figure. Thus the members of any one religious community have more or less totally ignored what has been said by and written about the other great figures.

For the times in which we live this is no longer appropriate. Like it or not, we are living in a world community, a "global village," in which we are increasingly made to be aware of and to relate to other peoples, peoples with different views of reality from those that our own traditions have given us. Some who encourage crosscultural understanding suggest that it is important to know *why* other peoples view the world the way they do—with the idea that if one understands, then one will know more adequately how to treat them, how to relate to them. But for many who encourage such an understanding in a pragmatic mode, the idea that one might learn something, that others might make a contribution to one's own vision, is unthought of.

There are also those who actively reject any suggestion that one might learn from beyond one's own traditional community. For

159

many the modern world in its complexity is so threatening that they want to retreat into a closed and secure world of the past. The evidence of such retreat is there in a key figure such as the Ayatollah Khomeini. But also, closer to home, there are Protestant Christian fundamentalists whose success in meeting the needs of a threatened and insecure America can be seen in the recent boom of their television talk shows and in the rise of the Moral Majority.

I find these movements disappointing, even disturbing: for I am convinced that we must push forward toward making our global community truly a community, toward developing a vision of our common humanity rather than of our divided humanity. The scenario of groups of persons living in walled cities of their own ideas, living in fear and suspicion of outsiders, is a depressing prognostication. The possibility that I want to explore, then, in the remainder of this work is that we might be able to come together from our different traditions and draw upon the wisdom and the vision of our breakthrough figures. There is a context in which this is possible and I shall attempt to elucidate it.

A key event for me in the attempt to articulate this context was a chance reading some years ago that the first portrait bust sculpted after the fall of Rome (which took place in 410 A.D.) was made in Florence in 1453 (Hah, 18–19). This fact led to the observation that since 1453 there has been an unprecedented interest in painting persons—realistically, impressionistically, expressionistically. The point of the observation is elucidated by a series of contrasts of *this* use of painting with the place of painting in other cultures: with Eastern Orthodox Christianity, for example, where paintings are icons, images of God; with medieval Catholicism where major pictorial representations were of saints and were presented, in the main, stylistically; with India, where traditionally almost all paintings and sculptures were of deities or avatars; with Taoists, in whose paintings persons are so blended into a landscape that one can barely see them; with the situation in communist countries where leaders are presented individually and realistically and the people collectively and stylistically; with traditional Jews and Muslims where paintings of human beings have been, in general, prohibited.

These contrasts led me to the conviction that one can learn

much about a culture from the ways in which its visual and plastic arts have treated human figures. That is, each of the approaches to painting that I have just mentioned is a kind of shorthand for an essential focus of the culture concerned. There is, for example, a clear tie between the story of Lao Tzu's disappearance into Tibet and the fact that one can barely see human individuals in a Taoist landscape painting—and the clue is that both portray a blending of the human into the totality of the harmonious movement of Tao. And in the Islamic case one can understand that the injunction against the portrayal of images of human and other living creatures is an expression of submission to God's greatness, to the unequivocal demand that God alone be the center and object of human reverence and worship.

The recent interest in painting human individuals as they really are reflects a new stage of human self-understanding—which is further expressed (in this era of Instamatic and Polaroid) in the interest that persons have in taking photographs of friends and family, in recording the stages of a child's life, in capturing central moments of the pilgrimage and experience of life. What that first portrait bust of 1453 indicates is a new focus—or a renewed one, for something similar can be seen in ancient Greece and Rome—on the significance of each individual, a fascination with human personality in all its vicissitudes, its terror and its greatness, its hopes and fears.[70] The contrast between the paintings of the early Renaissance and family photograph albums and home movies in every household of Europe and North America also tells us something quite important. In the earlier stages of this development the focus of attention was upon the aristocracy. But there has been a massive democratization, an elevation of the "common man" so that every person is the worthy subject of portraiture. Every American boy (though not yet every girl perhaps) can dream of being president of the U.S.A.

All of which leads me to assert that there is another great tradition beyond those related to the leading lights we have looked at—the humanist tradition. It is arguable that the humanist tradition is the most widespread tradition in the modern world; and it is found in a variety of forms. Within the broad context of this humanist movement there is considerable diversity and divergence. One can see at one extreme a Marxist humanism degenerating into its most striking and terrifying form in the Leninist-Marxist version of the Soviet Union; and at the other extreme a particular American vision, a democratic psychologism focusing on individual personal fulfillment.[71] Both of them are problematic, the former so obsessed with the state organization and control of human structures that individual freedoms are grossly limited—to the extent that we, looking on, are convinced of a serious *dehumanization*. On the other side, there is the kind of problem that one finds in populism: the populism of *People* magazine where the saints of the culture are ephemeral types, the stars of television and movies and rock music; where children in school can read trash and feel they are being educated; where the concern for *quality* in human life is lost;[72] where political leaders do whatever the polls tell them is most popular, without regard for issues of morality or truth or justice.

In part, one can get to this problem by thinking in terms of elites. The initial interest in humanism was an interest of a particular elitist group. As the humanist vision has developed there has been a radical rejection of the kinds of elitism evident when the humanist movement was just beginning. Few today would be happy with the idea of a ruling class whose natural privilege is to control society. The problem of elites, however, has not been solved as easily as one might have hoped; in Marxist societies, for instance, power elites have developed in such a way that the full richness and potentiality of human life has been seriously curtailed. In America there is the counterproblem that the leaders, the political elite, are beholden to a population that may understand very imperfectly what is necessary in the complexities of modern political life. Also, the ideal of personal fulfillment expressed in the American Dream has frequently taken the form of a blatant materialism, a clinging to *things*. It has proved to be a highly dynamic dream—but one that because of its drain upon the resources of the earth is also increasingly dangerous.

Both these versions of humanism indicate a crisis in the humanist movement. One can thus understand more easily the desire of many, as mentioned just above, to return to a traditionalist approach, to a life of quality, in which the old securities, the solid old moralities, are retained.

Yet this seems to me not to meet the problem. In the first place, as I have said, the withdrawal to the visions of the past rarely does justice to the circumstances of our present need for appreciation of our global heritage. Secondly, all the traditions as developed contain within them elements that have been shown to be problematic: the domination and degradation of women by men, the exploitation of the poor by the rich. Too close an identification with past traditions seems to lead inevitably to systems that are less humane; that, for example, keep women very solidly in second place, that restrict and repress.

That we are aware of the former difficulty is largely a product of this humanist movement. It might be observed that the very fact that we are able to do what we have done so far, to view sympathetically each of these great religious figures, is itself a product of the humanist tradition in which we participate. That we can look at human history in its various manifestations, that we can attempt to understand what has gone on in different cultures over the millennia, is the result of this humanist interest. But having been drawn on by this humanist interest to view the history of religion as one, we cannot be content with traditionalist theologies that tend to be parochial or, as John Hick has said it, "pre-Copernican" (see Hick, 125–32).

I should explain my use of the term "theology." The term derives from a Christian context where it has come increasingly to be interpreted as the attempt on the part of members of the Christian community of faith to give a systematic and exhaustive intellectual expression of what is involved in their faith. But members of other religious communities have attempted similar intellectual expressions. A useful alternative term might be the Indian word *darshana*, which is used for Hindu systems of religious thought. The word means "seeing, perceiving, vision" in both literal and metaphysical senses, but also "showing, exhibiting." In the context of Hindu systems of thought, *darshana* might be glossed as "insight or vision coming to intellectual expression"; yet one could take it a step further and talk of intellectual expression giving rise to liberating vision or insight.[73]

Given the humanist background of the descriptive, historical study in which we have been engaged, what I am arguing for is the *darshana* of a mature humanism—of a humanism that is not *naively* modern but is able to relate itself adequately to the human past. From the critical context with which we began—the inade-quacies of traditional Christian views of other religious commu-nities—the context in which we live drives us forward toward the *darshana* of a planetary humanism.

Drawing again on the Christian context, it seems to me most valuable to center such a theology/*darshana* on the concept of revelation. But then I believe we need to redeem the concept of revelation through an awareness that talk of revelation is merely another way of speaking about discovery.[74] Thus, for example, one might speak of human discovery of the nature of reality—from subatomic particles to galaxies, from the anatomy and phys-iology of the human body to the structures of human interaction through to the fulfillments of human living. But then one might place such discovery in a different perspective and talk of revela-tion, the self-disclosure of multifarious Reality to human expe-rience.[75]

But we have returned to our starting point. And here I should make more explicit the point of the word that I have scattered through this discussion and have used as the title for this book: breakthrough. These great religious thinkers broke through to discover and communicate a vision that has sustained and directed the lives of their followers. The breakthrough of the mas-ter made possible a breakthrough for the disciples into a life they found fulfilling and enhanced.

But "breakthrough" can be applied equally well to that "other side of the coin," revelation. The Reality of the universe broke through to the imagination of these remarkably creative persons in such a way that their lives are perceived by the followers as in some sense a conduit of the supremely Real into human expe-rience. As I have emphasized on a number of occasions, we can-not see the original breakthroughs. The records we have, the traditions handed down, are the record of a response, a witness to the breakthrough into the lives of the followers of the great orig-inal discoverers. The early followers have presented to succeeding generations, in the teachings and the mythic accounts of the lives of their teachers, the central elements of the original break-through. And the members of all religious communities affirm that through those records breakthrough still occurs.

It is this awareness of an original, powerful breakthrough, and the continuing breakthrough, that gives rise to what the members of the various communities have said about their leaders. Muslims have talked about breakthrough in terms of a verbal communication from God to the perfect receptor, Muhammad. Christians, many Hindus, and some Buddhists have, in varying ways, as I have tried to show, identified their breakthrough with that central "divine" Reality that has been disclosed to human experience.

I am suggesting, then, a theology of revelation, a *darshana* of breakthrough that enables us to accept the legitimacy of the central discoveries, insight, wisdom of all the traditions. But, in the light of such a vision, I also want to suggest that we take a further step and realize that our full humanity can be found in drawing upon the totality of our common human heritage—as demonstrated, initially, in the lives and teachings of our breakthrough figures. And I am encouraged by the fact that in the various life stories we have examined there are different modifications of the conflict and journey-quest motifs, for it suggests that in the interests of our full, global humanity we may complete the sacred circle by drawing these visions together.

How can this be done? The place to begin, I think, is to recognize that in the life stories and teachings we have examined there are similar interests expressed in different ways, in differing cultural contexts.

Most widespread is the interest in how persons are to live together in human community. The elements of the Buddha's teaching that refer to good conduct, the attempts of Kung-tzu and Lao-tzu to set forth a harmonious pattern of life for Chinese society, Hindu interest in dharma, and the centrally ethical focus of Jewish and Islamic religious patterns—all reflect this interest. There are, of course, different emphases in these systems. In contrast with the Confucian ideal of the polished gentleman, the man of finesse, the details of the Islamic ideal of submission to God seem almost fanatical. Moreover, there are differing emphases on stability and freedom, punishment and reward, love and justice, rights and responsibilities.

For the future of our global village we can do nothing better than consider seriously as points of debate these differing emphases. We have noted that Jews and Muslims developed methods for bringing the ancient word to the contemporary situation, and indeed all the great traditions developed such methods. Particularly helpful for our task is the view of the Jewish rabbis that it is via the effort of hard debate that the ancient word manifests itself as a living reality in the life of the community. For any community, a vital basis might be worked out in sharing as elements of debate the different positions provided by other communities.

I could look forward with some hope to a future in which, in critical and hard debate, the values of the past are allowed to speak to the needs of the future. I am not advocating an easy acceptance of these past visions. That would be impossible in any case for, as we have seen, there are discrepant views presented in them. I am convinced, however, that out of conflict and debate, we shall be able to put together a wiser future than if we either retreat to secure but limited visions from the past, or develop a naive humanism bereft of history.

It should be emphasized, however, that debate alone will not be enough. I would hope that, as a result of this debate, as members of the various religious communities become aware of their mutual concern for stability and security, justice and freedom, there would be a more practical drawing together—with representatives of the various communities working together in solidarity, vigorously and hardheadedly, for a more fully human life for all the peoples of our world.

Beyond the social setting, the life story and teaching of each of the foundational religious figures has something else to offer. One might talk about it in terms of a personal quest—though it is not always so focused. From another perspective one might think about it as a focus of interest on God or on Transcendent Reality—though again it is not always focused in either of these ways. That is, with the exception of Master Kung, each of these figures points to a Reality—beyond the social setting—of prime importance. All, apart from Krishna, are pictured as leaving ordinary life and going out into the wilderness. This shared event might be interpreted as a transcendence of the social dimension and of the flat reality of commonsense experience, and the discovery of a dimension of depth, of mystery. In general, the event is understood either as an encounter with a Being accepted as the central, significant Reality of the universe or as a discovery of a fulfilling, liberating way of life, or both. Each such foray provides for us a context for a social setting. Significant elements of the contexts differ but they are, I believe, not contradictory; they are complementary. Thus for Muhammad socio-political life is lived as submission to God, and many features of his system underline the importance of continually focusing one's life on God. In a more limited, "national" context, the life for Jews, the life of Torah, is their response as God's covenant people. In the stories of the childhood and youth of Krishna a similar message is mediated, for from it Hindus understand that human fulfillment is found in serving God with love and devotion—giving to God, in the form God takes in an image in temple or home, gifts such as one would offer to one's dearest friend or a supremely honored guest.

With Jesus, Lao-tzu, and Gautama one sees variations on the relationship between the individual and the universe, each of which provides a particular kind of input into the social setting. Thus Jesus' portraying of humankind as the children of God injects a creative new dynamic into human interaction as persons serve each other, loving each other as members of the same family. Gautama, in his uncompromising portrayal of the unclinging, selfless life, also brings this dynamic quality to social interactions. Both of these, as indicated in my utilization of a Zen story to elucidate Jesus' words, express the conviction that in an unclinging attitude toward the world and toward ourselves we can find a fulfillment of our humanity quite unlike anything that is possible from any other perspective. The portrayal in Lao-tzu of the harmonization of human society with the entire cosmic process is a message that is becoming increasingly welcome and increasingly heard, in the wake of recent concern about ecology. Lao-tzu suggests for us that a truly fulfilled humanity will be careful in its treatment of the resources of our world, will be sensitive to the cosmic flow.

I should emphasize that in drawing together these visions I am not here envisaging some new "super-religion."[76] That would be altogether too dull. Just as I would consider it a terrible impoverishment for our world if Canadians, Britons, Americans, Indians, Australians—all peoples among whom I have lived and whose cultural distinctiveness I cherish—became, say, one larger United States, so too it would be tragic if we all rejected the rich traditions of our religious heritage in the interests of syncretistic mix.

Consider what would happen in the area of ritual alone: just to try to produce a Hindu-Christian wedding ritual would be a formidable and ultimately unrewarding task. If one tried to combine the elements of both traditions the result would be a symbolic mess. If one decided to dispense with all distinctively Christian and Hindu symbols, the result would be a pale, colorless flow of words lacking symbolic depth.

I do not expect that we shall witness a new great teacher-hero with a single way for our times. Although we may still have our heroes, from Terry Fox to Gandhi, who in various ways capture our imagination and give us direction, and the details of whose lives fit somewhat into archetypal heroic journeys and battles against inimical powers, no one person is capable of drawing together all these strands. Moreover, modern psychological study has made it impossible for any modern hero to mediate fully a vision of help for our times. We know too much about ourselves. Albert Schweitzer turns out to have had paternalistic and patronizing attitudes toward the Africans among whom he spent much of his life. The glowing picture that Louis Fischer gives of Gandhi loses its glow somewhat when one becomes aware of Gandhi's rather quirkish obsessions with digestion and sexuality brought to light by Eric Erickson, Ved Mehta, and others.[77] About the great figures of the past we know too little to undercut the archetypal presentations of their lives; our modern heroes will all be of limited significance, and given the diversity and pluralism of our times, that is how it should be.

What, then, am I envisaging? On one wall of my university office I have a number of pictures—cheap prints, postcards, pages from books—of Jesus, Krishna, Gautama. A friend who teaches at the University of Kerala near Trivandrum in South India, and who was my tutor in Malayalam, has on his desk a piece of glass and beneath it postcard pictures of images of God from some of the major temples of South India. And there among them, is a picture of Jesus praying in the garden of Gethsemane. In symbolic terms, what my friend and I have done is, I believe, of great importance.

What I am suggesting is that, given the intellectual framework for understanding breakthrough that I have presented, it will now be possible for persons, although remaining thoroughly within the communities that mean so much to them, to enrich those communities with a vision from beyond. In practical terms this would mean the study by the members of a Christian congregation of other visions, beginning with presentations of the kind I have given here. It would imply a similar study in Hindu ashrams, Buddhist monasteries, Jewish synagogues, and other religious communities as well as in households and schools and universities scattered across the globe. But it would involve more than the merely intellectual effort that the term "study" suggests; it would mean an encounter in which our lives are touched by the playfulness of Krishna, the warm love of Jesus, the zeal of Muhammad, the finesse of Kung, the wit of Lao, the peace of Gautama.

The world awaits a new breakthrough, a new revelation, a new *darshana*, in the combined vision and wisdom of our great discoverers. Reality has broken through to human life and experience via these great creative figures and light has been shed on the pathway of human life. The times in which we live call for the directing of all the separate lights onto our common path. In the careful development of systems of social responsibility and freedom; in lives lived in submission to God; in lives lived with unselfishness and unclinging, in which therefore all the worlds in spontaneity and awareness and lucidity can be enjoyed—in such a vision there is hope.

A Vision for Women?

What I am suggesting here, in a global *darshana* of breakthrough and a sharing across traditional boundaries, is unusual enough to raise questions. First there is the problem that such a humanly shared *darshana* would have to take into account the extremes of Islamic theism and Buddhist atheism. This is not really a problem for us if we are able to acknowledge that in different historical contexts different views of reality have been developed—or, to put it differently, the self-disclosure of Reality has called forth different human conceptualizations. I can find no solid reason for judging one or another of these as final or superior. We may indeed be able to get to the point of seeing that what somebody else says on the question is a corrective, gives new depth to certain of our own conceptions.[78]

But that takes us into the other suggestion, that we might learn something significant from beyond our own traditions. Even in the recent past, most communities have been wary of this idea. Some scholars have ventured so far as to suggest that by studying another tradition one may be sensitized to themes hidden, perhaps, in one's own traditions. I have implicitly accepted the validity of this view by using, for example, a Zen story and a Hasidic story to elucidate the significance of Jesus. (An important corollary of my approach would be that Zen masters and Jewish Hasidic communities have themselves seen something rather similar to what Jesus is showing us.) And one can certainly see (to use some examples from recent Christian history) that, through an encounter with Hindu yoga and Buddhist approaches to meditation, many Christians have returned to a new awareness of Christian traditions of spirituality; and that others, learning of the significance of play and dance in Hinduism, have been able to see Jesus as a playful figure, as "Lord of the Dance."[79]

I am suggesting, however, something more radical than this. The view that one may be enriched with a vision from beyond is based on an observation of Gandhi's development of his idea of nonviolence and on my own encounter with Krishna via the Hindu tradition. It is arguable that Gandhi's reading of the Sermon on the Mount (informed by Tolstoy's interpretation) enabled him to refind the Indian teachings about *ahimsa*, nonviolence. Yet it seems clear that the idea of nonviolence that he developed was much more dynamic than that from his Indian heritage, much deepened by his encounter with the Christian idea of love. In somewhat similar fashion, I can indicate that my encounter with Krishna was related to my interest in the Christian theology of play. I came to see, however, in the mischievous child, the lively dance, the magic flute, a charming and playful quality that adds a new dimension to all that I have received through my Christian heritage (see Hospital, "Kṛṣṇa," 285-91). My encounter with the figure of Krishna constituted a kind of personal breakthrough, an epiphany of the divine that affects deeply my view of life and the universe.

Undoubtedly there are many difficulties that could be raised with respect to the idea of sharing between adherents of different groups. I do not imagine that I could be exhaustive in dealing with such questions; that would clearly be the work for another book or several books. It does seem to me worthwhile, however, to address one specific situation. My interest in doing this is occasioned by the observation of a friend of mine, who in looking over the suggestions of this final chapter wondered whether he could proffer them to the Jewish girls whom he teaches in his college classes. And it is true that they as a group raise two questions for us in a quite radical way. On the one hand there is the question of the relationship of modern women to these discoverers; on the other, and representing another pole of the problem, can you seriously ask Jews to be open to an encounter with Jesus?

On the first question, the issue is whether the life story and teachings of any of these figures can be the source of legitimate breakthrough for women in the late twentieth century; for they are all males, and they all display to some extent the fruits of patriarchy, a view of males as dominant and somehow more significant, more fully human, than females. Even Jesus, who, recent Christian scholars have been proud to note, was amazingly open toward women, treating them as full human beings—even he was not able to break from a picture of God as dominant male. He focused into the idea of God a certain intimacy from the family circle: "When you pray, say Abba, father . . ."—but it was the *fatherhood* and not the *motherhood* of God that he envisioned.

Some radical feminists have decided that the entire baggage of the major traditions from the past (including the foundational figures that we have presented) is so trapped in the patriarchal complex as to be unredeemable. In seeking an alternative approach two different paths have been followed. One of them attempts to seek out and resurrect the prepatriarchal traditions, those of the mother goddess. There is evidence of the presence of these traditions as a subculture or counterculture in many of the cultures we have been discussing: what needs to be done, the argument goes, is to refind them, to celebrate the feminine via these traditions.

Yet there is a problem here. From all the evidence we have— both from past records from the Middle East and Europe and from the continuing goddess cults in South Asia—goddess history is violent and bloodthirsty. There are accounts of the killing of humans as a sacrifice to the goddess, and large-scale animal sacrifices are remarkably widespread. It is dubious that anything other than a highly romanticized version of the goddess would be of help to women in our time.

The other path begins with contemporary experiences of women; if it looks at history at all, it sees significant history as going back little further than the suffragettes. The reason why this is problematic has already been touched on. A humanism—even a feminist humanism—bereft of history does not seem as likely to be what we need as one that plumbs the depths of past discoveries and draws fresh waters from the wells of wisdom. In addition, as I have said, I do not think that modern biographies can draw on and utilize the archetypal in the way our discoverers have done.

The question to which we return, then, is whether the breakthrough centered in these male figures can be, as I have said, the source of legitimate breakthrough for us all, female and male, at this point in our collective history. I think that they can be—that much of what is mediated by these figures, as I have attempted to portray them, applies as readily to a woman's humanity as to a man's.

I have also suggested, however, a new kind of hermeneutic for bringing the ancient vision to the contemporary scene in allowing the different emphases of these past visions of society as points of debate for our contemporary quests. But if we think more carefully about the significance of the contemporary scene in that process, we can see that the contemporary woman's quest for full humanity—like that of the contemporary poor of the "two-thirds world"—becomes a critical input into this hermeneutical process.

Let us think for a moment about what that critical input might effect. One result would be a new sensitivity to the part played by women in these breakthrough accounts. What is probably the primal hymn of the exodus is attributed to Moses' sister Miriam, who leads the women of the community in a dance and a hymn giving thanks to God for deliverance from oppression (Exod. 15:20–21). This is but the first of three great hymns of women in similar vein that derive from this heritage of Israel. The second is Hannah's hymn, the hymn of the barren woman who is so oppressed by patriarchal values. The hymn of joy occasioned by the birth of her son Samuel is fitted into the patriarchal mold—God renders her a blessed wife of the patriarchy after all! Yet a careful reading of the hymn brings to light a protest against all forms of oppression, an envisioning of the overturn of all oppressive systems:

> Those who had plenty sell themselves for a crust,
> and the hungry grow strong again.
> The barren woman has seven children,
> and the mother of many sons is left to languish.

> He lifts the weak out of the dust
> and raises the poor from the dunghill;
> to give them a place among the great,
> to set them in seats of honour [1 Sam. 2:5, 8].

Also clearly part of this heritage of Israel, and modeled on Hannah's hymn, is the hymn sung down through the ages by Christians, the Magnificat. This hymn of Mary is even more explicit in the envisioning of the overturning of oppression:

> He has brought down monarchs from their thrones,
> but the humble have been lifted high.
> The hungry he has satisfied with good things
> the rich sent empty away [Luke 1:52–53].

There is a suggestion of a similar breaking through the structures of privilege in the Krishna traditions. Poems in the *Krishna-karnamrita* (1.48; 1.94) make the point that the males who hug their lofty spiritual paths to themselves spend years looking for God without success—but God is revealed in all glory and beauty to the simple, loving women of a cowherd village.

Even more important as a contribution to hermeneutics are two stories—one about Gautama and the other about Jesus. We are told that one of the Buddha's lay followers, a woman, requested that women be admitted to the order of *bhikshus*. The Buddha at first refused; she persisted and eventually, persuaded by his disciple, Ananda, he agreed. The account is thoroughly mediated by the misogyny of the tradition (whether it was also the Buddha's own, of course, we cannot tell), for the Buddha is pictured as going on to predict that, as a result, adherence to *dharma*, his teaching, would not endure as long. But to focus on this misogyny masks the remarkable fact that the Buddha agreed to her request; for he could not deny that the path he had found was as legitimate for women as for men. Thus, the woman's request constitutes an important breakthrough in the awareness of the universal applicability of the Buddhist path (see Warren, 441–47).

More startling is the story of Jesus' encounter with a woman from the area that is today Lebanon. The woman requests that Jesus heal her daughter:

> Jesus then left that place and withdrew to the region of Tyre and Sidon. And a Canaanite woman from those parts came crying out, "Sir! have pity on me, Son of David; my daughter is tormented by a devil." But he said not a word in reply. His disciples came and urged him: "Send her away; see how she comes shouting after us." Jesus replied, "I was sent to the lost sheep of the house of Israel, and to them alone." But the woman came and fell at his feet and cried, "Help me, sir." To this Jesus replied, "It is not right to take the children's bread and throw it to the dogs." "True, sir," she answered; "and yet the dogs eat the scraps that fall from their masters' table." Hearing this Jesus replied, "Woman, what faith you have! Be it as you wish!" And from that moment her daughter was restored to health [Matt. 15:21–28].

I used to regard this as a story about "a woman's faith," as the heading in the *New English Bible* has it—a picture of faith as persistence: if we accept Jesus as God incarnate, her encounter models the persistence that human faith involves. If, however, we can allow ourselves to be creatively heretical, and see Jesus as human, all too human, then something else comes to light; for here is Jesus confining his mission to "the lost sheep of the house of Israel." This woman is clearly beyond the bounds of Jesus' understanding of his mission. She is an outsider. Yet her deep need renders her sensitive to the fact that the healing he brings is not something that can be confined in the way he claims. Her persistence involves an expansion of his vision, to the extent that at the end he is saying in amazement, "Woman, what faith you have!"

The significance of this story for our discussion is in its broadening of our perception of the way in which the breakthrough, the discovery, occurs. It encourages us to see beyond the *individual* in whom Christians have focused the "breaking through," to a situation of *encounter* in which the breakthrough takes place. One might say that in this case God is as much revealed through the woman as through Jesus. But this suggests that similar breakthroughs may occur as these discoverers are encountered by us today. In particular, as the women of our times articulate their questions and critiques, we may see these discoverers called to new understandings—beyond the limitations in which the male-dominated traditions have held them.[80]

One cannot but notice that the full humanity of women is in the interests of us all, male and female. Systems based on dominance rather than on mutuality are degrading to the dominant as well as to the dominated. I think of the situation in India, where generally men are placed in a position of responsibility over women throughout their lives. One of the offshoots of this system is that in order to effect a good marriage for his daughter, a father must provide for her economic well-being through a substantial dowry. Pity the man who has four or five daughters! They can bring him to economic ruin. Such a burden, apart from all the other positive valuation that patriarchy gives to sons, is sufficient reason why the birth of a son is an occasion of great joy, that of a daughter the occasion of some disappointment. Although this does not mean that women are unloved, it does suggest, deep down, an unnecessary tension between the sexes. It renders women second-class human beings, and gives to some men an intolerable burden of responsibility.

Jewish Openness to Jesus?

The second question—Can a Jew be open to an encounter with Jesus?—raises for us in more critical form a problem that has kept surfacing and is so distressing a part of Western religious history, that of the relationships between the various religious communities. Although we may now say that we must find a new relationship, is not the most we can ask a "live-and-let-live" kind of acceptance? Is it not true that the most we can do on many substantive issues is to agree to disagree? Or, to push things a bit further: When we look at certain communities—Jews, Christians, Muslims—even in the rather open style we have developed here, are there not clear contradictions inherent in the different visions of these traditions? Can Christians see Moses as anyone other than the foundational person of a superseded system, the old covenant based in Torah (and hence John 1:17: "While the Law was given through Moses, grace and truth came through Jesus Christ")? Can Jews accept Jesus as any other than a false Messiah? Can Christians be open to learning anything from Muhammad? Can Muslims see Jesus as any other than merely a prophet whose work has been superseded by the full and final vision given by God via Muhammad?

In part the issue here is our initial problem of an exclusiveness that becomes attached to ways that are seen as universal. When the writer of John has Jesus say, "I am the way . . . the truth . . . the life," he is presenting a strong conviction that he and millions of other Christians have shared. But the clause that he adds: "No one comes to the Father except by me," does not necessarily follow and, it has often been pointed out, does not seem quite consistent with the Christian picture of a loving parent-God whose love embraces the whole world.

In considering a somewhat similar statement—"There is no other name under heaven granted to men, by which we may receive salvation" (Acts 4:12)—Krister Stendahl suggests that like much religious language (particularly liturgical or confessional language) this is "love language." He uses the following analogy:

> If a husband were to say that his wife was the only one for him, and he were telling the truth and nothing but the truth, then that is good and true. But if he were witnessing in court under oath and the judge asked him whether he could be sure that nowhere in the world could there be another woman about whom he could have come to say the same thing, then he could not take such an oath. For in that setting the very same words would take on another meaning [Anderson and Stransky, 18].

The point is that by using the negative mode, by denying any other possibility, one maximizes one's affirmation. But if such statements are taken as literal and dogmatic truth, it must surely be seen as an insult to the legitimacy of other people's experience.

A critical point in the relationship between Jews and Christians has to do with the relationship between Torah and what Jesus has done. Both John, as noted above, and Paul in his picture of Torah as a tutor or baby-sitter (above p. 152) suggests a striking discontinuity. Yet it is blatantly false to much of the tradition of Israel not to see the context of Torah as that of God's covenant love or grace. That Paul was not able to see this may tell us more about him (and perhaps about others like him in the Pharisaic community) then it tells us about the long-standing traditions of Israel.

Another critical point in the relationship between Jews and Christians has to do with the identification of Jesus as the Messiah. Here the actual disagreement is much clearer; and the point of our question—Can Jews be open to an encounter with Jesus?—becomes much sharper.

Tom Driver has recently suggested a reconsideration by Christians of the picture of Jesus as the Christ. He argues, in a style reminiscent of Albert Schweitzer, that Jesus was looking forward to the coming of the messianic age, did not see himself as the Messiah. He also makes the point that to see Jesus as the Christ is a stumbling block to relationships with Jews, for he wants Christians to be able to stand together with Jews in the affirmation that the Christ is yet to come.[81]

There is some point to this, for Christians have had to take certain elements common in the Jewish Messianic tradition—the pictures of a messianic age of peace and concord, free of sorrow, the desert bursting into flower (after Isa. 35)—and transpose them to the future, to the time when Jesus returns. Yet the tradition that Jesus was the Messiah seems to be too deeply embedded in Christian tradition to be easily excised.

Are we left, then, with a position that either Jews or Christians are in error? Or is it possible that both are right in their own way? It seems clear that if one looks at Jesus from the perspective of the people of Israel collectively, Jesus was not the Messiah. The vision of the messianic age was not realized. Yet for some, what they saw and experienced in the life of Jesus—the breakthrough that was occurring—had to be expressed in terms of messianic imagery. (Later, as I have indicated, in other contexts, other ways were developed for speaking about what had happened.)

If we can see, then, that the identification or nonidentification of Jesus as the Messiah depends upon crucially different perspectives, then we may also go ahead to see the full legitimacy both of the movement that became the Christian church—those who saw Jesus as the Messiah—and of the continuing community of the Jewish people.

Does that mean—I return to the question again—that Jews cannot be open to an encounter with Jesus? There does not seem to be any inherent reason why Jews cannot see Jesus as a breakthrough figure. Yet when Christians look at what has been done to Jews down through nearly two thousand years in the name of Jesus, they can only acknowledge that it would be an insult for a Christian to suggest such an encounter to Jews. All Christians can legitimately do, it seems to me, is to ask forgiveness, offer a hand of friendship, and stand side by side with Jews in the quest for justice and freedom for all peoples.

And should any Jews be open to an encounter with Jesus, the attitude of a Christian might well be informed again by the story of Jesus and the Canaanite woman.

Jesus was amazed at her faith. That in itself is amazing, for it is doubtful that she saw Jesus as the Messiah—the more primitive version of the story in Mark makes no such suggestion—and it is highly unlikely that she believed in God in the terms with which Jesus was familiar. But also surprising is that, aware of her faith, Jesus did not say, "Now come—become a Jew and join my band of followers." Jesus was more Jewish than his Christian followers have been in allowing that God works in God's own way with the peoples of the world. All that happened—all that happened!—was that her daughter was healed and she went on her way into the Lebanese countryside.

Jesus was able to hear this woman from outside his community, was able to have his own vision expanded by hers. He was able to respond to her cry for help. He was also able to allow her to accept the healing he had to offer on her own terms—and leave it there, except for an amazed affirmation of her faith! Can any of us from among our modern communities do more than that for our sisters and brothers?

NOTES

1. For a full discussion of the idea of "founders," see Wilfred Cantwell Smith, *The Meaning and End of Religion,* New York, Mentor, 1964, 112–17.

2. See, e.g., John Hick, *God and the Universe of Faiths,* London, Macmillan, 1973; John B. Cobb, *Christ in a Pluralistic Age,* Philadelphia, Westminster, 1975; idem, *Beyond Dialogue,* Philadelphia, Fortress, 1982; Raymond Pannikkar, *The Unknown Christ of Hinduism,* London, Darton, Longman & Todd, 1964; Paul Knitter, *No Other Name?,* Maryknoll, N.Y., Orbis, 1985.

3. I heard this in a lecture presented some years ago. He has included the discussion in chap. 1 of his *Towards a World Theology,* Philadelphia, Westminster, 1981.

4. The first four verses of the Gospel of Luke indicate an interest in giving an accurate account of the events of the life of Jesus. The author says that those who have written accounts of Jesus' life have "(followed) the traditions handed down to us by the original eyewitnesses and servants of the Gospel" (Luke 1:2), and he presumably sees himself as following the same policy. There is, however, no indication on the part of the author of whether he attempted to determine the authenticity of traditions or whether he was even aware of the question of authenticity. Certainly there is no suggestion that he is following the methods of historical research standard for a modern historian.

5. For a recent discussion of this question of historicity and a suggestion that literary criticism may be more important than historical criticism in understanding the biblical text, see Charles Davis, "The Theological Career of Historical Criticism of the Bible," *Cross Currents,* 32 (1982) 267–84.

6. From *The Dhammapada,* translated from the Pali by P. Lal, New York, Farrar, Strauss and Giroux, 1967.

7. For an indication of the extent of the Pali canon, see Richard Robinson, *The Buddhist Religion,* Belmont, Cal., Dickenson, 1970, 125–27, and Kenneth K.S. Ch'en, *Buddhism,* Woodbury, N.Y., Barron's Educational Series, 1968, 215–24.

8. The Indian doctrine of rebirth is accepted as axiomatic by writers of these materials.

9. That the future Buddha dwells in one of the highest heavens fits the general pattern of Indian thinking about rebirth. One of such virtue will naturally be brought by that virtue to one of the highest heavens.

10. "Angel" also means "messenger"—see below, chap. 5.

11. This is often referred to as Indra's net. The mythology of orthodox Hindus, including the conception of various superhuman beings, gods, and the like, is accepted also by Buddhists.

12. The importance of the horoscope can still be seen in modern India. The range of cosmic forces at work at the time of the birth of a child is considered of great importance as a prognostication of future success in marriage, business, etc.

13. The Buddha is called by various names, one of which is Siddhartha, meaning "he whose aim has been accomplished, he who has reached his goal."

14. For a recent discussion of such questions, see Roy Amore, *Two Masters: One Message,* Nashville, Abingdon, 1974.

15. The Buddha was somewhat indirectly influential in the Western world at a later date through the teaching of Mani. See Hans Jonas, *The Gnostic Religion,* Boston, Beacon, 1963, 206-9.

16. Examples of such hero figures range from Gilgamesh in the ancient Mesopotamian Epic of Gilgamesh, through Greek heroes such as Theseus who slew the Minotaur, and Heracles (Hercules) who overcame numerous dangerous beings, down to the Christian dragon slayer, St. George.

17. Gilgamesh is an example in his search for the plant of immortality; again there are examples from Greek heroes such as Jason; and there are numerous stories of Christian knights searching for a special treasure, of which the best-known example is the cycle of King Arthur and his Knights of the Round Table.

18. Some kind of ritual response to this transcendent quality appears to date from the time of Mount Carmel man, 200,000 to 100,000 B.C. Wilfred Cantwell Smith sees in the burial practices evidence that "man from the very earliest traces of his beginning has recognized that there is more to human life than meets the eye, that the total significance of man is not exhausted within the six feet of space or sixty years of time with which he plays his part on the stage of earth" (*The Faith of Other Men,* New York, Mentor, 1965, 21-22.) An actual concept of an element that survives death, a living center, a soul, comes to its earliest expression in the thinking of the Egyptians.

19. I was given these details by friends who lived nearby and showed us around Forest Lawn.

20. For a further helpful discussion of *dukkha,* see Wilfred Cantwell Smith, "Religious Atheism? Early Buddhist and Recent American," *Milla wa-Milla,* 6 (1966) 9.

21. From the well-known hymn of Isaac Watts, "O God Our Help in Ages Past."

22. See Robert E. Hume, trans., *The Thirteen Principal Upanishads,* London, Oxford University Press, 1931.

23. One might relate this back to the discussion of desire or craving. Although it is not spelled out in these terms, *tanha* is effectively *selfish* desire. And clearly desirelessness or freedom from craving does not mean a directionless fatalism. The Buddhist way is a quest focused in a transcendence of egocentric clinging.

24. See *Chandogya Upanishad,* 6.9–6.16 (Hume, 246–50).

25. For a discussion of a specific form of this in the situation of war, see Ernest Becker, *Escape from Evil,* New York, Free Press, 1976, 106.

26. One should perhaps note that this is not a quietistic or "otherworldly" ideal. It does not imply insensitivity to the suffering of others. The story of the Buddha's return to share what he has found, and the importance of the virtue of compassion *(mehta, metta),* attest to quite dynamic implications in this vision of peace.

27. These translations are my own, as are those of all other citations in this chapter that are not given a translation source.

28. Within different systems different terminology is used. For Buddhists and Jains the central term is *bhikshu,* a wandering beggar, often translated "monk" because for large parts of the world they lived together in communities that could be called monasteries. The term *sannyasin* is more common among Hindus, and is a more broadly descriptive term, for it is applicable to all who have left the ordinary style of life and have moved out to live a life focused on the search for the Self, for liberation.

29. There is considerable debate about whether this is first found in literary form in the *Bhagavad Gita.* Much depends on the dating of different texts, and that in itself is beset with problems. What is perhaps most significant is that a *bhakti* phase appears to have developed almost simultaneously among orthodox Hindus and among Buddhists, and with it a much stronger emphasis upon the legitimacy of the life of the ordinary person as way toward liberation.

30. It is almost certain that a number of different writers had a part in the composition and final form of the *Gita,* and the lack of clarity in the relationships between the various paths is probably affected by it.

31. In the *Rig Veda,* however, deities at times break out of their limitation to specific phenomena and are addressed in much more cosmic terms. Max Müller referred to this as "Kathenotheism."

32. Much of what is said of Krishna in the *Gita* is reminiscent of statements about Brahman, the supreme reality of the Upanishads. See Franklin Edgerton, trans., *The Bhagavad Gītā,* New York, Harper Torch Books, 1944, 146–54.

33. For a brief discussion of the dating of these Puranas, see Wendy Doniger O'Flaherty, *Hindu Myths,* Harmondsworth, Middlesex, Penguin, 1975, 16–18.

34. For a further discussion of this, see my article "Līlā in the Bhāgavata Purāṇa," *Purāṇa,* 22 (1980) 4–22.

35. Translations of 2.7, 7.1, 7.18, and 11.11 are from William Theodore deBary et al., *Sources of Chinese Tradition,* Columbia University Press, 1964, pp. 27, 23, 20, and 29. Those of 8.2, 12.21, and 17.11 are from D. Howard Smith, *Chinese Religions,* New York, Holt, Rinehart and Winston, 1971, pp. 41–42. Those of 10.9, 12.2, and 18.6 are from Arthur Waley, trans., *The Analects of Confucius,* New York, Vintage, 1938, pp. 149, 162, and 220.

36. We in the modern West have recently tended to accept as axiomatic some form of the "equality" myth. It is not yet clear that it is the most appropriate to the conditions of human life. It is important, at any rate, to acknowledge that we still live by hierarchies, largely those of economic power, and to allow the ideals of others like Kung to help us to think more critically about our ideals of equality, and about the kinds of hierarchies that we want to work/fight for.

37. The word "midrash" is derived from a Hebrew word from a root meaning "to ferret out." It is frequently translated "exegesis," and it refers essentially to the task of explaining what a biblical passage means. The term is the more appropriate with reference to Chuang-tzu in that the midrashes of the rabbis have often involved similarly earthy stories.

38. It is perhaps worth noting that the Mahayana development of the idea of the nondifference of nirvana and *samsara* fits rather well with the Taoist view of Tao, in that in both cases significant reality is perceived not as some entity transcending the world, but rather in terms of the world itself.

39. See, e.g., John 18:21–31; 19:12–16. One might also note that even earlier, in Mark and Matthew, the predominant responsibility for the death of Jesus is placed on Jews: Caiaphas, the high priest; the chief priests in the Sanhedrin; the crowd, persuaded by the chief priests and elders, that asked for the release of Barabbas and the death of Jesus. In the synoptic Gospels, however, these are not lumped together as *hoi Iudaioi,* "the Jews" (as in John).

40. It should be noted in passing that modern scholarship has raised the question of the historicity of Moses in perhaps as radical a form as that of Krishna or Lao Tzu. The historical evidence suggests that some of

those who later looked back to Abraham and Moses were descendants of nomadic tribes that spent some time in Egypt (referred to in Egyptian writings as the Hyksos) but had then been forced out of Egypt. On the question of whether there was a historical figure, Moses, who was responsible for effecting the escape from Egypt, there is no independent evidence.

41. See *Peake's Commentary on the Bible,* Matthew Black, ed., London, Thomas Nelson, 1962, 212–13, for a brief discussion of the word and scholarly opinion about its meaning.

42. See R.C. Zaehner, *Hinduism,* New York, Oxford University Press, 1966, 23; and the discussion by Thorkild Jacobsen in H. Frankfort et al., *Before Philosophy,* Harmondsworth, Middlesex, Penguin, 1949, 184–98.

43. "Go Down, Moses" has been printed in numerous versions. One of the earliest is that in J.B.T. Marsh, *The Story of the Jubilee Singers,* Melbourne, Mason, Firth and M'Cutcheon, 1886, 142–43.

44. I have tried to avoid using the word "Jews" to refer to the ancient people, using rather the word "Israel" or "Israelites," derived from their ancestor, Jacob, also called Israel. The word "Jew" is from the Greek *Iudaioi,* the inhabitants of the Roman kingdom of Judea (in Greek, *Ioudaia),* derived from the Hebrew name for the land, Judah (lit. Yehudah). This is in turn derived from the division of the people of Israel into two kingdoms, Israel and Judah, in 933 B.C. After the northern kingdom of Israel fell to the Assyrians in 721 B.C. and its inhabitants were scattered throughout the Assyrian empire, the people of Judah became the bearer of the heritage of the people of Israel. It should be emphasized that Jewish persons have rarely thought of themselves as "Jews" even in modern times. They have continued to identify themselves as the nation or people of Israel.

45. For a discussion of the Talmudic Age, see Leo Schwartz, ed., *Great Ages and Ideas of the Jewish People,* New York, Modern Library, 1956, 174–83.

46. From a different method of distinguishing the ten words of the Decalogue, Catholic Christians have divided them into three relating to God, and seven relating to the people. This is not, however, the Jewish division.

47. The picture of the creation of the world by Yahweh as given in Gen. 2 may be dated to before 900 B.C.E. (see Gerhard von Rad, *Genesis,* London, SCM Press, 1961, 23). But a sophisticated grasping of the connection between God's activity in creation and God's work in history is first evident in Deutero-Isaiah (see *The Interpreter's Bible,* Nashville, Abingdon, 1952–1957, vol. 5, p. 408).

48. The importance of the second journey, the journey of the people,

can be seen in the major cycle of Jewish festivals datable from biblical times: Pesach (Passover) commemorates the escape from Egypt; Shavuoth (Pentecost), the giving of the Decalogue at Sinai; and Sukkoth ("booths") commemorates the forty years of wandering in the wilderness.

49. The translation is that of N. J. Dawood, *The Koran,* Harmondsworth, Middlesex, Penguin, 1959. It seems to me to provide the best combination of felicitous English prose and intelligibility.

50. It should be emphasized that the Arabic word *Allah* is cognate with the Hebrew word translated into English as "God." And it seems to me essential to understand that when English-speaking Christians talk of God and Muslims speak of Allah, they are not referring to different beings. Not that their views of God are identical; but then there is considerable variety even in Christian views of the nature of God.

51. E.g., the well-known English traditional Christmas carol known as "The Cherry Tree Carol" where the baby speaks while still in Mary's womb and the cherry tree obeys his command by offering Mary its fruit.

52. See Wilfred Cantwell Smith, *The Faith of Other Men,* New York, Harper & Row, 1972, 53–66, for a thoughtful treatment of the Creed.

53. I have not explored in depth the question of relationships between the sexes. All of the major traditions here represented have been more or less male chauvinistic. I am not convinced that that invalidates the central visions they have communicated. It should also be noted that the final word on the validity of the modern vision has not yet been spoken: some versions of a mutually manipulative "equality" may be no more helpful than the traditional forms from the past. It does seem to me, however, that once we have been sensitized to the ways in which women have been rendered second-class human beings, we can never go back to the old systems of male domination. At the same time practical expression of the modern sensibility will likely be wiser if it draws creatively on past traditions. (For further discussion of this final general principle, see chap. 6 below.)

54. It might be argued that I have in the Islamic case overplayed the emphasis on praxis rather than belief or doctrine. It has been noted that there seems to be a greater flexibility about doctrine within Judaism than in the Islamic case; there does not seem to be any equivalent to Reform Judaism in Islam. It seems to me, however, that the issue here is not a matter of flexibility—or inflexibility—concerning doctrine, except at one point. The flexibility of Reform Jews is in the area of praxis, and it has been developed on the basis of modern views of the development of the human species throughout history. What was put together as the injunctions of Torah several thousand years ago is seen to contain much that cannot apply to our age, much that is a product of a more primitive age.

(Orthodox Jews, of course, disagree radically with this perception.) Muslims have much greater difficulty applying such a developmental-historical approach, for they see the giving of the Quran as a final and complete self-disclosure of God. And the traditional view of the Quran takes into account the more primitive quality of earlier messages. The accepted teaching that Muhammad was unlettered and had no part in the quranic revelation other than being a receptor of the divine message—such an effective doctrinal safeguard of the full legitimacy of the Quran—stands as a major block to the asking of critical questions about the origins of the contents of the Quran.

55. See 1 Cor. 10:1–12 and Acts 1:1–24. Forty days may be a pointer to the forty years in the wilderness. The coming of the Holy Spirit on the day of Pentecost (the Jewish festival of Shavuoth, commemorating the giving of Torah) draws on the proclamations of Ezek. 37 and Jer. 31:31–34.

56. The more usual translation is "kingdom of God." The concept, however, appears more dynamic than the word "kingdom" indicates. It is God's kingly rule, a divine activity to which those invited may or may not respond.

57. In the version in Matt. 14:22–33 there is added an account of Peter's attempt to walk on the water, which becomes the basis of a short discourse on faith and an indication of Jesus' power to uphold and sustain.

58. Mark 3:18 refers to "Simon, a member of the Zealot party." Some scholars have conjectured that Judas too was a Zealot.

59. The first line of a well-known hymn by John Keble.

60. I should say that I am gratified to discover that some recent New Testament scholars have been suggesting something similar to what I am attempting to elucidate by the comparison with Zen *koans*; see Robert C. Tannahill, *The Sword of His Mouth,* Philadelphia, Fortress, 1975.

61. For a discussion of this *koan,* see Robert Linssen, *Zen: The Art of Life,* New York, Pyramid, 1972.

62. See also the discussion on pp. 9–10.

63. I am indebted initially to the Rev. Ronald Noble of the First Baptist Church in Kingston, Ontario, for this insight. A similar view is argued at length in James P. Mackey, *Jesus the Man and the Myth,* New York, Paulist, 1979, 94–120. There is a like discussion in Hans Küng, *On Being a Christian,* Garden City, N.Y., Doubleday, 1976, 343–86.

64. The accusations of blasphemy in Matt. 26:59–65 and Luke 22:66–71 are quite unclear on this. Jesus frequently called himself the "son of man," although it is difficult to say just what that term implies. There seems little doubt that he acquiesced in his disciples' view of him as the Messiah, though he appears to have been intent on giving a different view from the view popular at the time, of the Messiah as a political

figure. The term "son of God" is used not by him but by his accusers. There is no indication whether he accepted their accusation and what is to be understood by it.

65. For the use of this delightfully enlightening translation, I am indebted to Dr. Robert Osborne of Carleton University.

66. For a discussion of Rom. 3:25, see F.J. Leanhardt, *The Epistle to the Romans: A Commentary,* London, Lutterworth, 1961.

67. Recent critical scholars have generally been in agreement that this Gospel was not written by John, the disciple of Jesus, but by a pupil of John who wrote the Gospel after John's death. For a full discussion of the problem of authorship of this Gospel, see C.K. Barrett, *The Gospel According to St. John,* London, SPCK, 1958, 105-14.

68. See Barrett (n. 67), 34-45.

69. In Hindu tradition, *darshana* refers to a sighting or a showing of God. Most often it is applied to the encounter of devotees with a deity in the temple, where the deity deigns to take form in an image. The mode of *darshana* also fits the portrayal of Krishna (above, p. 61) surrounded by his devotees, for whom his presence and form are an act of grace.

70. One might see Shakespeare as the first great literary representative of this tradition, with the rise of the novel as a further stage.

71. For a discussion of this, see Philip Rieff, *The Triumph of the Therapeutic,* New York, Harper & Row, 1968, and Christopher Lasch, *The Culture of Narcissism,* New York, Norton, 1979.

72. The issue of the quality of life is raised in Robert M. Pirsig, *Zen and the Art of Motorcycle Maintenance,* New York, Morrow, 1974.

73. Note that I have used the word above in the context of the sighting of an image of God, the unveiling of the glory of God. The context I am now drawing on is different, but it is valuable to remind ourselves of the continuity in Indian terminology between the vision of God and the vision of an intellectual system.

74. For this basic idea I am dependent on a passing reference by Peter Berger in *A Rumor of Angels,* Garden City, N.Y., Doubleday Anchor, 1970, 82.

75. I have been eager here to point to a continuity between religious and scientific discovery because I regard as one of the more tragic aspects of our recent history the commonly held view of a radical dichotomy between revelation as a religious mode and discovery as a scientific mode.

76. It will be observed that I am suggesting two rather different approaches at the theoretical and the practical levels. I am advocating a meta-theology that arises out of and is sensitive to the wide-ranging history of human religiousness. It will need to be of such a kind that it will allow the long-standing symbols of the various traditions to remain via-

ble. At the practical level, I see people continuing to relate primarily to their traditional symbols.

77. See Louis Fischer, *Gandhi: His Life and Message for the World,* New York, Mentor, 1954; Eric Erickson, *Gandhi's Truth,* New York, Norton, 1970; and Ved Mehta, *Mahatma Gandhi and his Apostles,* Harmondsworth, Middlesex, Penguin, 1977.

78. See Paul Tillich, *Christianity and the Encounter of the World Religions,* Columbia University Press, 1963, chap. 4; and John Cobb, *Beyond Dialogue,* chap. 4 and 5.

79. For an account of something similar vis-à-vis the Islamic tradition, see Wilfred Cantwell Smith, *The Faith of Other Men,* New York, Mentor, 1963, 82. One should perhaps observe, in relation to the discussion below on Jews and Jesus, that it is likely that there will be little in what Jesus presents that is not already there in Jewish tradition in some form.

80. I am encouraged in this hope by some of the fine work being done by feminist theologians—in particular, as a recent example, Rosemary Radford Ruether, *Sexism and God-Talk,* Boston, Beacon, 1983.

81. See Tom Driver, *Christ in a Changing World,* New York, Crossroad, 1981, chap. 1.

WORKS CITED

Akhilananda, Swami, *Hindu View of Christ,* New York, Philosophic Library, 1949.

Anderson, Gerald, and Stransky, Thomas F., *Christ's Lordship and Religious Pluralism,* Maryknoll, N.Y., Orbis, 1981.

Andrae, Tor, *Muhammad: The Man and his Faith,* New York, Harper Torch Books, 1960.

Arberry, Arthur J., *The Koran Interpreted,* London, Oxford University Press, 1964.

Barth, Markus, *The Broken Wall,* Chicago, Judson, 1959.

Bodde, Derk, "Myths of Ancient China," in *Mythologies of the Ancient World,* Garden City, N.Y., Anchor, 1961.

Buber, Martin, *Tales of the Hasidim: The Early Masters,* New York, Schocken, 1947.

Bynner, Witter, *The Way of Life according to Laotzu,* New York, Capricorn, 1962.

Campbell, Joseph, *The Hero with a Thousand Faces,* Princeton University Press, 1968.

Conze, Edward, trans., *Buddhist Scriptures,* Harmondsworth, Middlesex, Penguin, 1959.

Cross, Frank M., "The Song of the Sea and Canaanite Myth," in Herbert Braun, *God and Christ,* New York, Harper Torch Books, 1968.

deBary, William Theodore, et al., *Sources of Chinese Tradition,* Columbia University Press, 1964.

Dimock, Edward C., Jr., *The Place of the Hidden Moon,* University of Chicago Press, 1966.

———, and Levertov, Denise, *In Praise of Krishna,* Garden City, N.Y., Anchor, 1967.

Douglas, Mary, *Purity and Danger,* Harmondsworth, Middlesex, Penguin, 1970.

Eliot, Sir Charles, *Hinduism and Buddhism,* London, Routledge and Kegan Paul, 1921.

Guillaume, Alfred, *Islam,* Harmondsworth, Middlesex, Penguin, 1956.

Hah, John R., *Renaissance,* New York, Time-Life Books, 1965.

Hertzberg, Arthur, *Judaism,* New York, Brazillier, 1961.

Hospital, Clifford, "Krṣṇa and the Theology of Play," *Studies in Religion/Sciences Religieuses,* 6 (1976—77) 285-91.

Hume, Robert E., trans., *The Thirteen Principal Upanishads,* London, Oxford University Press, 1931.

James, E.O., *History of Religions,* London, English Universities Press, 1956.

Khan, Muhammad Zafrulla, *Islam: Its Meaning for Modern Man,* London, Routledge and Kegan Paul, 1980.

Linssen, Robert, *Zen: The Art of Life,* New York, Pyramid, 1972.

Mellinkoff, Ruth, *The Horned Moses in Medieval Art and Thought,* University of California Press, 1970.

Merton, Thomas, *The Way of Chuang Tzu,* New York, New Directions, 1965.

Nasr, Sayyed Hossein, *Ideals and Realities of Islam,* New York, Praeger, 1966.

Radhakrishnan, Sarvapalli, and Moore, Charles A., *A Sourcebook in Indian Philosophy,* Princeton University Press, 1957.

Rahman, Fazlur, *Islam,* Garden City, N.Y., Doubleday Anchor, 1968.

Reps, Paul, *Zen Flesh, Zen Bones,* Garden City, N.Y., Doubleday, n.d.

Rodinson, Maxine, *Mohammad,* Harmondsworth, Middlesex, Penguin, 1973.

Rupp, Gordon, *Last Things First,* London, SCM, 1964.

Smart, Ninian, *The Long Search,* Boston, Little, Brown, 1977.

———, *World Religions: A Dialogue,* Harmondsworth, Middlesex, Penguin, 1966.

Stewart, Desmond, *Early Islam,* New York, Time-Life Books, 1967.

Thielicke, Helmut, *How the World Began,* Philadelphia, Muhlenberg, 1961.

Thompson, Laurence G., *Chinese Religion: An Introduction,* Belmont, Cal., Dickenson, 1969.

Waley, Arthur, trans., *The Analects of Confucius,* New York, Vintage, 1938.

———, trans., *The Way and Its Power,* New York, Grove, 1958.

Warren, Henry Clarke, *Buddhism in Translations,* New York, Atheneum, 1963.

Watts, Alan W., *Myths and Ritual in Christianity,* Boston, Beacon, 1968.

Welch, Holmes, *Taoism: The Parting of the Way,* Boston, Beacon, 1965.

Wright, Arthur F., *Buddhism in Chinese History,* New York, Atheneum, 1965.

Zaehner, R.C., *Hindu Scriptures,* London, Dent, 1966.

Zimmer, Heinrich, *Philosophies of India,* London, Routledge and Kegan Paul, 1951.

Other Orbis Books . . .

NO OTHER NAME?
A Critical Survey of Christian Attitudes
Toward the World Religions
by Paul F. Knitter
Might other religions be as valid as Christianity as a means to know God?
Is Jesus Christ unique among the savior figures of the world? Are the
many religions all equally true? How should they relate to each other? In
dealing with these and other questions of religious pluralism, Paul Knitter, Professor of Theology at Xavier University, Cincinnati, proposes a
bold "theocentric, non-normative" understanding of Christ.

"This is first-rate creative theology. . . . It is also written to serve as a
college textbook and succeeds in this admirably. At the same time,
theologians will find it very enlightening, if not downright revolution-
ary." *Leonard Swidler, Temple University*

Item no. 347 *304pp. Paper*

PLURALISM
Challenge to World Religions
by Harold Coward
A clear and comprehensive treatment of the attitudes of each of the great
world religions to the others. Masterful chapters on the way Judaism,
Christianity, Islam, Hinduism, and Buddhism have reacted and are react-
ing to the challenge of religious pluralism are followed by a new set of
guidelines for interreligious dialogue. Essential reading for anyone interested in communication across religions.

". . . a valuable new resource, filling an important gap in the literature."
John Hick, Claremont Graduate School

Item no. 710 *144pp. Paper*

BUDDHISM MADE PLAIN
An Introduction for Christians and Jews
by Antony Fernando with Leonard Swidler

Sri Lankan author Antony Fernando has overcome a massive challenge—namely, to present an understandable, meaningful explanation of the heart of Buddhism and to compare it to the heart of the Judeo-Christian tradition. A superb introductory text for college students and lay study groups, this book will also claim the attention of experts on Buddhism.

Item no. 198   *176pp. Paper*

EASTERN PATHS AND THE CHRISTIAN WAY
by Paul Clasper

"This is a sensitively and well-written book on one of the most significant issues of our day, ecumenism among world religions."

Catholic Library World

"Worthwhile for the informed layperson with an interest in ecumenical dialogue."   *Library Journal*

Item no. 100   *144pp. Paper*

GOD'S CHOSEN PEOPLES
by Walbert Bühlmann

"Explores and reinterprets the theme of election, examining it from biblical, historical, comparative religion, and theological viewpoints. Bühlmann's basic thesis is that election and covenant theology are not exclusive to Israel or Christianity; other peoples often have similar convictions about their own desiny. Only when election of *all* peoples is understood does the message of revelation come clear."   *The Bible Today*

Item no. 150   *320pp. Paper*

THE SEARCH FOR GOD
An Encounter with the Peoples and Religions of Asia
by Walbert Bühlmann

"A journalistic introduction to the new phase of Christian mission and presence in the non-Western world, this work provides insight into the movement in Christian witness away from traditional missionary triumphalism to a new form of witness by presence and dialogue. The author sketches in brief reports on meetings of Catholics and Protestants in such diverse places as Bombay, Beirut, Manila, Nagpur, Bangalore, and amidst tribal groups in Indonesia and the Philippines. He gives brief insights into the theological work on the relation of Christianity to other religions by Rahner, Samartha, Küng, Panikkar, and others."

Theology Today

Item no. 450   *224pp. Paper*

PARTNERS IN DIALOGUE
Christianity and Other World Religions
by Arnulf Camps

"This text offers a convincing case that interreligious dialogue stands alongside liberation theology as one of the most urgent challenges and promising sources of renewal for contemporary Christianity. The author endorses mainline Roman Catholic approaches to other religions and shows the fruit it is bearing in the formation of local churches with new identities and theologies."   *Paul F. Knitter, Xavier University*

Item no. 378   *288pp. Paper*

COURAGE FOR DIALOGUE
Ecumenical Issues in Inter-Religious Relationships
by S. J. Samartha

"This collection of papers now becomes a primary source for historians of the ecumenical movement. . . . These essays are a great pleasure to read, clear in analysis, lucid in style, and marked often by a certain acerbic wit."   *International Bulletin of Missionary Research*

Item no. 094   *172pp. Paper*

CHRISTIANS AND RELIGIOUS PLURALISM
Patterns in the Christian Theology of Religions
by Alan Race

Alan Race probes deeply into the underlying theological questions by analyzing the numerous Christian responses to the new awareness of the world's richly varied religious history.

There are surveys of the three main explanations of the relationship between Christianity and the other religions given through their chief

proponents: those ~~who~~ ~~Christ~~ excludes other religions; those who hold that Christ is in some measure already present in
other religions; those who count the different religions as independently
valid communities of faith. As the doctrine of the Incarnation is pivotal
in the whole debate a chapter is devoted to recent discussion of it, and a
final chapter explores the question of truth in relation to inter-religious
dialogue.

Item no. 101   *192pp. Paper*

WITHDRAWN

LIVING FAITHS AND ULTIMATE GOALS
Salvation and World Religions
edited by S. J. Samartha
"This series of nine papers explores the question: 'What is the ultimate
goal of human life?' The nine contributors represent differing religious
and ideological persuasions: Christian and Hindu, Jew and Muslim,
Buddhist and Marxist."   *Theology Digest*

Item no. 297   *136pp. Paper*

THE EXPANSION OF GOD
by Leslie G. Howard
"An Irish Protestant now living in Asia, Howard is interested in the
meeting of East and West and in the dialogue between Christianity and
the Asian religions. Howard is no detached observer, for his aim is 'a
theological reinterpretation of Christianity which is more relevant to
Asian needs,' and he calls for a de-Westernized Christianity that 'will
become more like Hinduism and Buddhism' and will provide 'the basis
for a new kind of Christian culture or aesthetic.' "   *Choice*

"This may be one of the outstanding books on religion in the '80s. It is
refreshing, provocative and substantial." *The Daily Telegraph, London*

Item no. 121   *464pp. Paper*